DEVOTIONS
FROM THE EARTH

• Lessons From God in Nature •

LINDA S CARTER

The Lessons of Nature

Job 12:7-10 TVT
But ask the animals, and they will teach you,
or the birds in the sky, and they will tell you;
or speak to the earth, and it will teach you,
or let the fish in the sea inform you.
Which of all these does not know that
the hand of the Lord has done this?
In his hand is the life of every creature
and the breath of all mankind.

*This work is dedicated to Papa God
and the Holy Spirit who gave me endless
inspiration and insight to share these
words from an authentic and
heartfelt place.*

What People are Saying:

"One thing that sets these devotionals apart is its focus
on the natural world."

"I have so appreciated the author's insight into her heart and
her love of God's beautiful creation."

"Excellent writer. Linda captures the beauty of Gods
creation beautifully!"

"She impressed me in her simple childlike captivation with
the beauty of every item she sees in nature."

"A warming of my heart. This is the best way I can
share what I feel..."

"The book is wonderfully written and highly recommended as a
guide for morning meditations."

"This is a beautiful book."

"Easy, beautiful, lovely ... this devotional was a joy to read."

About This Book

Devotions From The Earth, Lessons From God in Nature is a compilation of four works in the series, each segment written for a six-week devotional journey. The beauty of nature is rediscovered as God's voice. This compilation extends for 24 weeks. Our companion journal will give you ample room for recording your notes and thoughts as the Spirit speaks through these writings each week. Journaling is optional, but so beneficial. If you don't do any writing, simply spend some time reflecting and praying about the readings each week.

The Weekly Reading Plan

This reading plan will allow you to do the short daily readings over a five day span, giving you some extra time to reflect and do some journaling on the sixth day. This routine suggests that you to do daily readings Monday through Friday, have some time to journal and reflect on Saturday, then take a break on Sunday as you meet with other believers. Ask the Holy Spirit to confirm or expand on things you've read during the week at your home church.

I recommend taking some time on Saturdays to get out into nature (even if it's just your backyard) to skim over the last five readings, talk to Papa about what he wants you to learn, and jot down some notes in your journal. Make this a time of solitude to listen and learn with your favorite blend of coffee or tea.

Contents

Contents

Mountains

INSPIRED BY NATURE'S BEAUTY

Introduction

The Earth has music for those who listen.
~George Santayana

Throughout history, mountains have captivated the hearts and minds of people. I personally find pure delight in nature and things created, and mountain landscapes are the most intriguing to me.

In this devotional, we will explore the mountains by delving into their spiritual significance to uncover the lessons they teach us about our faith and our relationship with God.

My inspiration for this book came when I moved to northern California, to a small rural community and bought a cabin in the woods on the ridge of a mountain. I had always dreamed of living in a pine forest. Living in this beautiful, wild place has given me an appreciation for the things of nature that I've never had before. I was moved to write down these notes that really are a picture of my devotion to all He has given us on the Earth, and to share with others the lessons and beauty to be found.

I hope these pages will encourage and inspire you to slow down a bit and take another look at how the Earth tells us it's story, and how it all reflects the creator. He has so much to say to us through His creation!

So soak in the panoramic views and wildlife images on each page. Lean into the scriptures, personal stories and reflective questions. Glean the lessons from the mountains that guide us toward deeper intimacy with God.

Mountains
Week One

Healing Mountains

Nature is our teacher, the divine force that can help
guide us towards a path of healing.
~*The Wellness Station*

Proverbs:16:24 TPT
Nothing is more appealing than speaking beautiful, life-giving
words. For they release sweetness to our souls and inner
healing to our spirits.

Healing experts agree that there is something about spending time in nature that is healing to our minds and bodies. Part of the reason that works is because it gets us away from stresses and pressures of life, and gives us a peaceful setting to recover. Nature brings us closer to our Creator. The things God made have a built-in design to heal themselves, and nature helps us get back in tune with that same design by which we were made.

But it's not just our minds and bodies that need healing. Sometimes our spirit being, the deepest part of what makes us who we are, is wounded. Things of the spirit can only be healed by the Spirit. I love the scripture above that teaches us how beautiful, life-giving words can release a sweetness to our souls and bring inner healing to our spirits.

Recently I went through a class that had us form small groups and do an exercise of asking the Holy Spirit for encouraging words for the people in our group, and then speaking those words over them. Then we prayed to seal those words so they would accomplish what God sent them to do. I have to say, I walked away from that class feeling lighter and inspired, with confirming words to tell me I was on the right path. It is amazing how our words, when combined with the guidance of the Holy Spirit, can heal and direct. Do you know someone who needs inner healing? Try asking the Holy Spirit for words of encouragement to speak.

Holy Spirit, I ask you for more encouraging words to share with those you put across my path. Help me to speak those words in spirit and in truth, and help those words be received to bring inner healing. Amen

Royal Cedars

The clearest way into the Universe is
through a forest wilderness. — *John Muir*

1 Kings 7:2 NIV
He built the Palace of the Forest of Lebanon a hundred cubits
long, fifty wide and thirty high, with four rows of cedar
columns supporting trimmed cedar beams.

I 've always loved pine forests, and had never been in a cedar forest until earlier this year when we were looking to buy a house in a new state. I was immediately in love with the lacy leaves and stately shape of these trees. If I always wanted to live in a forest, I never imagined it could be a cedar forest! The cedars on my property are very tall, with beautiful red bark and fragrant wood. No wonder cedar wood is so coveted for building special things - even kings palaces! What a joy to live among them.

When was the last time you recognized your Father's special gifts? Sometimes We ask for things, and then forget about them. It may be years later that we are suddenly aware that God did answer our prayers! Sometimes it wasn't even a prayer, it was just a simple desire in my heart. It's those moments that take my breath away and move me to tears as I recognize the gifts of the Lord in my life. It feels like I just noticed my Father winking at me.

Answers to prayer can be so subtle that we can miss them. Take a moment today to look around and see if you can recognize anything in your life that represents an old prayer or a desire in your heart come true that you might have missed. It might be something very small, or hugely big, but when you see it, you'll know... He just winked at you!

Father, open my eyes to see the little gifts and surprises you have placed in my life. I don't want to miss a thing! Thank you for the secret things in my heart that you have always known about me, and for answers to prayers. Amen

9

The Mighty Oak

Think of the fierce energy concentrated in an acorn!
You bury it in the ground, and it explodes into an oak!
— *George Bernard Shaw*

Isaiah 61:3 NIV
Beauty instead of ashes, the oil of joy instead of mourning, and a garment of praise instead of a spirit of despair.. They will be called oaks of righteousness, a planting of the Lord for the display of his splendor.

You might be surprised at all the references to oak trees in the Bible. Some of my favorite passages talk about the "mighty oak", which seem to represent well the black oak trees on my property. Because they are growing among the tall pines and cedars, they grow extremely tall as well, competing for the sun at the top of the canopy. Many oaks that the local power company has cut down in our area are almost hollow, and I wonder how the trees ever survived like that. They are sturdy and determined trees that hang on to life even as their insides are dying. I was examining a cut out of one of our oaks and it mesmerized me for a time to study the character of the wood. The rings spoke of many good and bad years, and the cracks spoke of an extremely dry season that was upon the tree at the time of its' death. In places the bark was gone and a fibrous growth covered up the wound. These trees are resilient.

No wonder God's word speaks so often about them, using them to teach many life lessons. He compares the righteous person to a tree planted by streams of water (Psalm 1:3). I believe that when we are planted in the Lord's family, we become more resilient to the world's harshness. So when things seem hard, I need to remember and even speak out loud that the Lord calls me an "oak of righteousness", and I am a planting of the Lord to display his splendor. What a beautiful thought to distract me from a momentary spirit of despair.

Thank you Father, for calling your scriptures to my mind when I need them most. Help me to hide more of it in my heart, so I can be refreshed and redirected by your words. Amen

Grassy Fields

Flourish: Flur•ish
1. To grow well or luxuriantly, Thrive
2. To do or fare well, prosper
3. To be in a period of highest productivity or excellence

Psalm 72:16 NLT
May there be abundant grain throughout the land, flourishing
even on the hilltops. May the fruit trees flourish like the trees of
Lebanon, and may the people thrive like grass in a field.

G rass is one of the most resilient growing things on planet Earth. As I write this, it's the beginning of winter, and the rainy season where we live. We have been so surprised and pleased to see the grass on the hills greening up like an early Spring. It had been such a dry, hot summer - the rain is so welcome; an answer to prayer. The rain brings everything to life again.

It reminds me of how the Holy Spirit is like a refreshing rain in our lives that brings freedom and life to the dry places. When we feel dull and lifeless, we must seek the presence of the Lord.

A few years ago I was in a spiritual dry spell. One day my husband stumbled upon a worship set online that stopped me in my tracks. I dropped everything and worshiped for forty five minutes, ending on my knees and in tears as I was drawn into the presence of God. "That's what I'm hungry for!" I said to myself. I began watching the online services from that church, a thousand miles away, and I wanted more. It sounds crazy to uproot my life and move across the country to go to a church that feeds my spirit, but it began to feel like a 'calling'. A year later we relocated to northern California to follow that call. This is home. This is where we can flourish and thrive. We came to find out that we weren't the only people hearing the call. Others from all over the world were coming to this place!

Thank you Father for the dry times that make us hungry for more of you. Holy Spirit, come to us in those dry times and fill us up again. Lead us to where we need to be, to flourish and thrive in both our physical and spiritual lives. Amen

Earth Rhythms

In every walk with nature one receives
far more than he seeks. *~John Muir*

Psalm 96:11-12 TVT
Let joy be the earth's rhythm...
Let all the trees of the forest dig in and reach
high with songs of joy before the Eternal...

Most people have favorite seasons of the year. I have found that my favorite seasons can change with where I live. When I lived in the desert, the summer months were agonizingly hot, and the perfect time for a get away. Living on the east coast, I loved the colors of fall. Today, living on a mountain ridge in an oak/pine forest has given me a new wonder for all seasons, as I learn how to read the finer points in the rhythms in nature. The way the wildlife comes and goes, the dry and wet weather patterns, the grasses and moss greening up with even the slightest bit of rain. I can almost sense the joy in nature that comes with small changes and rhythms.

When I recently came across Psalm 96, I felt my heart leap! It made so much sense to me that JOY is the Earth's rhythm. I started speaking it over my trees... "Dig deep! Reach high, and praise the Lord! Let joy be your rhythm!"

Can we speak encouraging words like that over our own lives? I think we can. I think we should. Gods' Word is a powerful force when spoken with conviction and faith. I encourage you to find a scripture that touches your spirit and start speaking it over your life. Dare to believe in the promises spoken over you, even if it's you doing the speaking. Look for (and expect) the joys that come with the rhythm of Gods' Word speaking into your spirit at times that only he knows you need it.

Father, thank you for your Word - an endless source of life and encouragement. Help me to embrace the rhythms of your promises as they apply to me day by day, moment by moment. Amen

Week One Reflections and Journaling Points

Write your reflections of the readings from the last week.

<u>Healing Mountains:</u> *How can we encourage others?*

<u>Royal Cedars:</u> *Special gifts or prayers answered.*

<u>Mighty Oak:</u> *Becoming an 'Oak of Righteousness'.*

<u>Grassy Fields:</u> *God's refreshing rain in a dry place.*

<u>Earth Rhythms:</u> *Speaking encouraging words over your life.*

<u>Other Reflections</u>

Mountains
Week Two

Mountains Majesty

You are not in the mountains. The mountains are in you.
- *John Muir*

Situated high above, Mount Zion is beautiful to see, the pleasure of the entire Earth. Mount Zion, in the north...

From my kitchen window is a breathtaking view of Mount Shasta. I never get tired of it. I always catch my breath when I see it. When the clouds obscure it, I sigh. What an amazing gift we've been given. All the beauty of creation, and the insight and passion to be able to appreciate it.

There's a saying, "Stop and smell the roses," which reminds us to slow down and appreciate the beautiful things that are right in front of us. I spent a lot of years in a busy, stressful blur of work, raising my daughter, running a business, etc. It took so long to break out of that cycle.

Simply taking a few minutes reading daily devotions will give us the pause we need to pursue the quiet moments that bring us closer to God. But more than just a pause, we need to recalibrate. Psalm 39:6 says, "In truth, each of us journeys through life like a shadow. We busy ourselves accomplishing nothing, piling up assets we can never keep..."

Lord, help us to have wisdom in knowing what is truly important in life. Teach us to live in the sweet space of appreciating everything you've given us every day. Help us find what it is you would have us do. Life is too precious to live like a shadow. Amen

Eagles Wings

When a storm is coming, all other birds seek shelter.
The eagle alone avoids the storm by flying above it.
So, in the storms of life may your heart be like
an eagle's and soar above. ~*Anonymous*

Isaiah 40:29 & 31 TVT
God strengthens the weary and gives vitality to those worn down by age and care.... those who trust in the Eternal One will regain their strength. They will soar on wings as eagles. They will run; never winded, never weary. They will walk, never tired, never faint.

The first day we arrived at our new home in the mountains, we saw an eagle soaring right over our property. It was such a blessing for us, and especially for my husband, because he has a special place in his heart for the Eagle. It was like a *sign* if you will, of God showing us we had arrived.   Our journey was finally completed. That eagle sighting on that day really gave us new strength after the long hard process of buying/selling/moving and finally landing at our new place to call home.

The birds in this area are completely different than what we were used to at our old house. Instead of finches, robins and sparrows, we have eagles, hawks, vultures and turkeys. Some days you can catch the big majestic birds soaring over our property in all their glory. Everything is different here, which was exactly what God had in mind for us.   It felt like we had been promoted, but little did we know, that with promotion comes more responsibility, trials and tests. We didn't know what trials were ahead, but the eagle sighting helped us know we were where we needed to be, and that God was with us.

Sometimes God speaks in unusual ways. Try opening your heart to allow him to speak to you in unconventional ways. Listen for his voice in beautiful and surprising things. He loves to give us those confirmations and little "hugs".

Father, I don't want to miss your voice in the little things. Help me to have ears to hear, and eyes to see what your Spirit is saying. Amen

Secret Places

Mountains know secrets we need to learn. That it might take time, it might be hard, but if you just hold on long enough, you will find the strength to rise up. *~Tyler Knott*

Psalm 16:11 TVT
You direct me on the path that leads to a beautiful life. As I
walk with you, the pleasures are never-ending, and I know true
joy and contentment.

Part of our property is on a steep mountain ridge, where you can easily find solitude and quiet on a short (although strenuous) walk through the forest. I cleared a small path that leads to my *secret place* and put a couple of comfortable chairs there. It's a special place that I can go to get centered in the tough times, have quiet meditation in spiritual moments, and take friends to have quiet, reflective talks.

These secret places can be very defining moments in our lives. It's where we get quiet enough to allow the Holy Spirit to lead us on the correct path of life, directing our thoughts and decisions, showing us truth from the lies, and giving us convictions to move ahead.

If you don't already have one, I encourage you to find your own secret place. A place where you can be still and listen for the Lords voice.

Thank you Father, for giving me quiet times of reflection to slow down and seek your wisdom so I can confidently walk the paths that lead to the true joy and contentment you have for each of us. Amen

Surefooted Deer

The more I see of deer, the more I admire them as mountaineers. ~ *John Muir*

Psalm 18:32-33 NLT
God arms me with strength, and he makes my way perfect. He makes me as surefooted as a deer, enabling me to stand on mountain heights.

It's been amazing to watch the wildlife come and go in my backyard. Over time they have gotten more and more comfortable with us. I now have a critter corner setup with water and nibbles, and some of them will even come running when they hear me calling, to see what goodies I've put out for them. The deer are the most gracious and beautiful creatures coming to visit by far. After months of watching them, I am amazed at how alert they are and yet how comfortable they can be when they know there is no present danger. They can jump and run so quickly when they sense alarm, flying down the mountain and never tripping up on the forest floor or the steep terrain.

They present a beautiful lesson on being relaxed enough to let go of tensions and anxieties when we have done all we know to do, while at the same time being ready to move when the time comes for it. It takes total trust in our God (and a little patience), to do that. How often I've had to force myself to take a deep breath and let go of things I have no control over, or to wait for answers instead of forcing them. I continually have to give my worries to God and take my mind and hands off of things. I believe that the more we do that, the less we'll have to. It's okay to let go. Give your worries to the Lord. Go forward as surefooted as the deer. We can trust that our Father is working everything out for our good.

Thank you Lord for arming me with strength and making my way perfect. Help me to be so comfortable with my trust in you that I walk and run without stumbling, just like the deer. Amen

Mountain Storms

Clouds come floating into my life, no longer to carry rain
or usher storm, but to add color to my sunset sky.
~ *Rabridanath Tagore*

Psalm 107:29-30 NLT
He calmed the storm to a whisper and stilled the waves. What a
blessing was that stillness...

Storms in the mountains can be absolutely magical. Sometimes our house on the mountain ridge sets us right in the clouds, like living in the "misty mountains". The sun pokes through now and then to make rays of golden light.

The rains can be hard and steady, or gentle and soaking. The snow is quiet and fluffy. Some storms come in with great gusts of wind that shake off the dead leaves and pine needles. This can leave a mess to clean up, but when the storm passes, the trees are so fresh, clean, and sparkly. The forest seems to perk up afterwards with new growth and color.

Maybe that's the way we should look at the storms in our lives… they are a part of life that is not always bright and sun shiny, but necessary to water the deep, dry seasons and help us navigate to a clean fresh new beginning. Yes, there may be damages to clean up, but with the Lord's help we come out on the other side ready to turn the corner, and go on to whatever is next. Without the prompting of the storm, we might not move at all, and miss out on new and better things that God has for us.

Lord, help me to not fear the storms so much. Help me to remember you are there to help me through every one… ready to still the waves and lead me on to better places. Amen

Week Two Reflections and Journaling Points

Write your reflections of the readings from the last week.

Mountains Majesty: About pausing and recalibrating.

Eagles Wings: How does God speak to you in unusual ways?

Secret Places: Plan your next quiet time in your secret place.

Surefooted Deer: Is there a worry you need to trust God with?

Mountain Storms: Is a storm navigating you to a better place?

Other Reflections

Mountains
Week Three

The Nature of Wisdom

Look deep into nature, and then you will understand
everything better. *~Albert Einstein*

Psalm 119:98-99 NLT
Your commands make me wiser than my enemies because they are always with me, I have more discernment than all my teachers because I study and meditate on Your testimonies.

If we pay attention along this journey called life, we learn lessons and become wiser and more discerning as we grow. It may take a lot of trial and error, but the lessons are there. Life is a great teacher, but I feel like I found the real treasure of wisdom and discernment in the Bible; God's Word and love letter to us. It's such an amazing and insightful book, which has spoken to me on literally every aspect of life.

So many of my "sabbatical" road trips end up in a mountain forest. It's not that the forest gives the wisdom, as much as it's the special place where I can "be still and know" my Father. It's where I can be inspired by what is created, because all of it points to him. In that state of mind, and in the special quiet places where beauty is all around, I tend to be able to listen and "hear" better.

If you're looking for answers but find that life doesn't slow down long enough to have quiet time with God, I recommend taking an overnight sabbatical trip to get away from everything so you can listen in the quiet of nature. The mountains and the forest are my favorite place for that.

Thank you, Lord, for always answering our prayers for more wisdom. Thank you for your Spirit that gives us discernment. Help us to quiet ourselves long enough to really listen and learn. Amen

A Forest Home

Forests are like churches, hallowed places. There's a
stillness about them, a sort of reverence.
- *Sabrina Elkins*

Psalm 104:16-18 TVT
The forests are Yours, Eternal One. Stout hardwoods watered
deeply, swollen with sap, like the great cedars of Lebanon you
planted, where many birds nest. There are fir trees for storks,
high hills for wild goats, stony cliffs for rock badgers. For each
place, a resident, and for each resident, a home.

The wild places of the Earth are beautiful, and the wildlife that lives in the mountain forests are fascinating to watch when you can spy them. Cities are for people. We are only visitors in the forest, although we sometimes carve out places to call our own. God made a place for everything to live. How special it is to live among the wild things.

The does and bucks wander through my property like they own it (actually, they do!). The blue jays and smaller birds come to help themselves to seeds the turkeys leave behind. Then the squirrels and rabbits started coming to see what might be there for them. The deer like to come for the bird seed, apples and carrots. A doe and her baby look for my treats regularly. And the turkeys roost in the trees on my property sometimes. How sweet to share the forest with them.

Let's never lose our childlike wonder for the things of creation. When we see how nature works in harmony for every living thing, we can know it's not an accident. It's intelligent design by a loving, very creative God. Take a breather from man made cities and visit the forest once in a while to remember the wonder of nature. The wonder of creation.

Thank you, Father, for the beauty of nature and wildlife that shows us what an amazing God you are. Help us not to lose our childlike faith. Amen

Mountain Birds

Be as a bird perched on a frail branch that she feels bending beneath her.. still she sings away all the same, knowing she has wings. ~*Victor Hugo*

Psalm 50:11 NLT
I know every bird on the mountains and all
the animals of the field are mine.

Some birds and animals you can only see in the mountains. To get a glimpse of a soaring eagle or a white owl is so special and rare. The wild turkeys have been coming around by the dozens to my clearing behind the house, What fun it is to watch their antics as they go about their scratching and searching for food. They are big beautiful birds - and a real treat to see them open up their feathers in full display. I started sprinkling bird seed for them, and over time they have become almost friendly, making a cooing noise when I come out with the seeds.

All this beauty belongs to the Lord. We are only stewards as he sees fit to give us what ever small part he thinks we can handle. The scriptures tell us that when we do well with the small things, he will give us more responsibility. My pastor once taught that more responsibility *is* the reward the Lord gives. Years ago I worked my way through a very difficult workplace situation with integrity. The only way I could do it was remembering that I don't work for men, I work for the Lord. That experience led to starting my own business, and I'm sure that was the reward for doing my best, even for a demeaning, hotheaded boss. Those days were filled with so many prayers for that man, and for my own patience! In the end, God actually used that man to help me get started being my own boss! I have to laugh at how that worked out... He really does work all things together for our good.

Thank you for the challenges and tests, Lord, they always lead us from glory to glory when we follow your ways. You are a good God. All the time. Amen

Mountain Songs

Sing a new song unto the Lord; let your song be sung from mountains high. Sing a new song unto the Lord, singing alleluia… *(Song by Dan Schutte)*

Isaiah 42:10-12 NIV
....Sing a new song to the Eternal... The peaks of mountains,
too, raise your voices with a great, glad cry. Let them all give
glory to the Eternal. Let them praise the One who is,
was and will be heard along the coasts.

We write songs about singing to the Lord on the mountaintops, and the Lord writes songs about the mountains themselves singing to him with great glad voices! Somehow the mountains, and in fact all of creation know their Creator. "Let all creation rejoice before the Lord..." (Psalm 96:13) Sometimes I can see rejoicing in the simple beauty of a flower blooming, giving it's all for the Lord. There was a day when people were born knowing our Creator, but that all changed many thousands of years ago in the Garden of Eden. Now, we are born into adversity and must search for him as for hidden treasure to know him. It's not automatic for us to find our Creator any more, but this is our destiny.

"All creation waits in eager expectation for the children of God to be revealed." (Romans 8:19) The "children of God"... that's us - the people who do find the hidden treasure of Jesus. What an amazing picture: all creation is watching the plan of the Lord unfold for us, his children, waiting for us to be revealed. In the waiting, all creation raises their voices to praise the God of creation. Even the angels watch in expectation; helping us along the way, and rejoicing when each one of us turn our hearts to God and welcome him in. (see Luke 5:9-10) Now we are also waiting for all to be revealed. We know the truth, and it has set us free, but there are so many others that are lost. We must help them find this treasure as well. This is also part of our destiny.

Lord, thank you for opening our eyes and hearts to know you. Show us how to work with you in guiding others to find the treasure of Jesus. Amen

Note: Stephen Curtis Chapman wrote a beautiful song called "The Treasure of Jesus" which you can find on YouTube.

37

Hiding Places

Right before I gave up, You saved me, You saved me. One
night you fell down from the stars, shining a light into the dark,
and you picked up all my broken parts.
(You Saved Me Song lyrics by Jake Miller)

Psalm 40:2 TVT
He reached down and drew me from the deep, dark hole where
I was stranded, mired in the muck and clay. With a gentle
hand, He pulled me out to set me down safely on a warm rock;
He held me until I was steady enough to continue
the journey again.

The mountain forests are beautiful, inspiring, and a wonderful place to seek the Lord to get centered. Sometimes on my worst days they provide a hiding place from life's pressures. Did you ever feel like you want to run away from everything? Yeah, me too. Now I know that running away doesn't solve anything, but sometimes a "get away" is just the ticket to take a breather and get with God about some serious business going on in my life. When my problems are caused by my own mistakes, they can be the hardest to overcome.

But the Lord is faithful to help me find myself, my beautiful self, again. Spending alone time with God helps me remember who I am in him. Just like the scripture above says, he pulls me out of my own mucky muck and helps me wash away all the bad feelings, forgive myself and others, and move on. Everyone has trials, and though they weigh heavy on us at times, we must face them, ask for forgiveness and let them roll off our shoulders.

In the book of Philipians, Paul says, "But one thing I do: Forgetting what is behind and straining toward what is ahead, I press on toward the goal to win the prize for which God has called me.." Living in the past and dragging our baggage with us doesn't work.

Papa God, thank you for always bringing me back from the muck and mire and setting me up on the high places, on the warm rocks, and holding me in your loving arms, listening to all my prayers, and drying all my tears, until I am ready to continue my journey again. Amen

Week Three Reflections and Journaling Points

Write your reflections of the readings from the last week.

<u>Nature's Wisdom:</u> *Reflect on spending time with nature.*

<u>Forest Home:</u> *Write about the wonder of creation.*

<u>Mountain Birds:</u> *How to be a better steward of God's gifts.*

<u>Mountain Songs:</u> *About your destiny in finding Jesus.*

<u>Hiding Places:</u> *Ask Papa God to pull you out of the muck.*

<u>Other Reflections</u>

Mountains
Week Four

Mountain Meadows

Cross the meadow and the stream and listen as the
peaceful water brings peace upon your soul.
~Maximillian Degenerez

Psalm 118:5-6 TVT
When trouble surrounded me, I cried out to the Eternal; He
answered me and brought me to a wide, open space. The
Eternal is with me, so I will not be afraid of anything.

The forest is pretty thick where I live, so it's nice to come across meadows when driving or walking about. Sometimes I like to pause and stay in the wide open areas for a few minutes. They somehow represent a safe place. Maybe it's because I can see more of what is in my immediate space. The sky is wide open, and I can relax.

When I found what Psalm 118 said about the "wide open spaces" being the Lord's answer to save people who are surrounded by trouble, I started speaking it when I found myself in any kind of trouble or dangerous place. When I feel backed into a corner by circumstances, or when I am out riding my motorcycle in rush hour traffic, I thank the Lord for 'wide open spaces'. There is lots of room to see clearly and get through what ever is causing me fear. It turns out that most times, the fear was the worst of the situation, and nothing bad ever happens. The Lord takes care of me and teaches me day by day to trust him more. Less fear, and more peace each time I speak out my faith in the middle of it. The next time you're afraid, try asking for your wide open spaces.

Thank you again, Lord, for your words that I can lean on when I need help. Thank you for wide open spaces to give me protection from the fearful things in life. If I had perfect faith, I might not fear at all, and you increase my faith a little more each time you turn my fear into peace. Amen

Deep Truths and Hidden Secrets

Go to the trees to explore your questions and dreams.
Go to the trees to desire and seek. The world will
listen as you walk, watch, soften and breathe.
~Victoria Erickson

Daniel 2:21-22 TVT
He gives wisdom to the wise and grants knowledge
to those with understanding. He reveals deep truths and
hidden secrets.

I have worked from home for thirty years, but I have never had such an inspiring view from my desk as at this house in the forest. When the deer and other wildlife wander through my property within view of the window, it can be hard to concentrate on work. Other times when I get stumped by some computer dilemma, I take a break and step outside or gaze out the window into the woods to gather my thoughts and clear my head. A quick prayer is the usual course of action, asking God to give me wisdom beyond my years to figure things out and do a good job.

Let's not forget how easy it is to glean wisdom from the Bible. In his book, The Wisdom of God, AW Tozer wrote: "We have degraded Christianity to be a kind of soft vaccine against hell and sin... The purpose of God in redeeming men was not to save them from hell only, but to save them to worship, and to allow them to be born into that eternal wisdom that was the Father." The back cover description for the book says, "Wisdom is not some highbrow philosophical concept, but rather a highly practical tool for living the best possible life." If we want to have the best possible life, we just need to find and apply God's wisdom. The hidden secret about all this is that it's so simple. Tozer taught from the scriptures of Paul that eternal wisdom was fulfilled in Jesus. Our journey to wisdom starts by deciding to follow Jesus. Is there anything hidden from you that you need wisdom to understand? Let's ask God for it…

Papa God, thank you for revealing deep truths and hidden secrets to us. Thank you for continuing to giving us wisdom for the every day details of life when we turn to you. Amen

Giant Redwoods

Count your age by friends, not years. Count your life by smiles, not tears. - *John Lennon*

The giant redwood forests are magical places. The first time I saw them I was awestruck. It was like I had been transported to a real enchanted forest you read about in The Lord of the Rings. There is a road called "Avenue of the Giants'"along the California coast that drives through the middle of a large giant redwood forest for miles. There are endless trails to walk among them with unusual giant ferns and clover along the path that I've never seen anywhere else. It's a wonder how they still exist in our time. Some have even been alive since the time of Jesus. Just think about what these old trees have seen and been through. But they hold on year after year to just be in the world for all to see and admire. If that is their only job, they do it well.

Are we ever too old to make a difference in the world? I don't think so. In fact, the older we are, the wiser we are, so we are far better equipped to mentor others or set an example. Older men and women can teach the young men and women how to live godly lives (see Titus 2). Even if you're still young, there will be someone younger than you to be a hero to. That's the way of the Kingdom, and there's still work to do.

Lord, help me to be the kind of person that can be used by you to be a godly influence to those around me... no matter how old I get. Amen

Walking in Love

The journey only requires you to put one foot in front of the other... again and again and again. And if you allow yourself opportunity to be present throughout the entirety of the trek, you will witness beauty every step of the way, not just at the summit. *Unknown*

1 Corinthians 16:14 TPT
Let love and kindness be the motivation
behind all that you do.

Walking mountain trails is so pleasing and refreshing. There are serious hikers who like the challenge of a hard climb and like to press in to make it to the tops of summits, and then there are folks like me who just like to meander along the easy green trails taking in the view. Every walk in the woods is like a little adventure in the journey of life. There is always new beauty to see and inspire.

When I lived in Phoenix some years ago, I used to get together with a couple of girlfriends for walks. We used to call them our "Walk of Faith" because it always turned out to be such a great time of ministry to each other as we shared the good and bad things going on in our lives. We rejoiced about the good things, or prayed for each other's needs. Fellowship with other believers is so sweet because we have that "kindred spirit" that brings us together in a shared faith, and in the love of Christ. It's also such a joy when others can see the love between us that makes an unexpected imprint on their hearts. Sometimes that is all it takes to plant a seed in an unbeliever's life. It's like a natural ministry that happens without us even trying. We just let our love and kindness for each other be seen, and it makes a difference.

Thank you, Father, that you don't waste anything. I pray you will continue to use me in natural and even unknown ways. Let my life be a testimony to you. Amen

Mountain Refuge

I always wanted to live in a log cabin at the foot of a mountain. I would ride my horse to town and pick up provisions. Then return to the cabin, with a big open fire, a record player and peace. - *Linda McCartney*

But blessings await all who trust in Him.
They will find God a gentle refuge.

If you've ever been to a cabin in the woods, you know what a special retreat they can be. When I was a young girl, I read a book called "My Side of the Mountain", which was about a young boy about my age (at the time) that ran away to the mountains. He lived in a hollowed out tree and made friends with the wildlife. I used to day dream of doing it too. What a great adventure that would be... or so I thought at the time. Now that I'm older and wiser, I can't imagine what a crazy scary idea that would be. I mean a cabin in the woods is one thing, but living in the wild, that is quite another. I am very thankful to have a strong, sturdy home to be safe and secure in the world.

But in this life, there is more than just our physical safety to think about. If you've been awakened spiritually in even a small way, you know there is more. Our Father has put eternity in our hearts, and I know the only true safe and secure place is trusting in him. He protects us in this life, and the one to come. He is the place our hearts and souls can take refuge.

Thank you, Lord, for giving us the sense to know you deep in our spirits, and to know that you have a plan for us. Thank you that we can know you are there for us to run to in every situation, and believe you will bring us to be with you one day. Amen

Week Four Reflections and Journaling Points

Write your reflections of the readings from the last week.

Mountains Meadow: Do you need safe, wide open spaces?

Hidden Truths and Secrets: A scripture that reveals truth to you.

Giant Redwoods: How can God use your talents?

Walking in Love: How can your love and kindness be seen?

Mountain Refuge: How can God be your refuge today?

Other Reflections

Mountains
Week Five

High on a Hill

For we must consider that we shall be as a city upon a
hill. The eyes of all people are upon us.
*John Winthrop dreams of a city on a hill; 1630 before
settlers reached New England*

Psalm 62:6
He alone is my rock and deliverance, my citadel high on a hill;
I will not be shaken. My salvation and my significance depend
ultimately on God; the core of my strength, my shelter, is in the
True God.

When I lived in Arizona, I used to visit the Grand Canyon on a regular basis. There is really nothing that can compare to the majesty of this place. There before your eyes is the most amazing landscape and evidence of Noah's flood we can find on planet earth. There are many secular arguments about how it was formed, but just from looking at it, my common sense agrees with creationists who say it must have been a cataclysmic event on a gigantic scale. First, you see all the different soils that were deposited in perfectly flat layers as the water was moving and swirling the earth in a global flood. Then to imagine the amount of water that must have been present to carve out the canyon as the water was receding. Together with volcanos and earth quakes, mountains rising and falling. What a crazy time for planet earth! But the evidence is there for all to see, so we are without excuse.

Today you can sit on the edge of the deep canyon high on a rock and gaze fifteen miles across to the other side. What a testimony of how beauty can come from ashes. That high rock gives us a vantage point that can make the whole event clear. It makes me think about the scripture above - how our Lord Jesus is our "Rock", our strength, our shelter. He sets us high on a hill with a great vantage point so we can see a bigger picture of what is going on in life, and not be shaken. Yes, there are things in life that will shake us up, initially, but that's when we gather our strength and look out from our vantage point and shake it off.

Lord I am in awe of the beauty you gave us here on planet earth, and how it all points back to you. Thank you for the strength you give us and the vantage point of seeing things from a heavenly perspective. Amen

Mountain Pass

Difficult roads often lead to beautiful destinations.
~Unknown

James 1:12 TPT
If your faith remains strong, even while surrounded by life's difficulties, you will continue to experience the untold blessings of God!

When I was younger, I was fearless about driving on mountain dirt roads that led to who knows where, on the edge of cliffs with no room to pass should an oncoming car come along. I really thought it was an adventure everyone would love, but I found out I was sorely wrong when I took my brother and sister-in-law (who were visiting from another state) on a 'scenic route' home from Cripple Creek, Colorado on a precarious back road. What started out as a fun outing, turned into a trip of horrors for my guests. My giggling about their fears (trying my best to make light of a bad situation) didn't help. It wasn't just a scary ordeal for them. I was suddenly someone they despised and wanted to get away from as soon as possible. They left for home sooner than planned. I felt horrible and sincerely apologized, but the damage was done.

Sometimes life can be difficult when unexpected things happen from bad decisions made. Even with no bad intentions, we still have to deal with the heartache of a wrong turn. It's easy to get depressed when things go wrong, and sometimes I allow myself to wallow in that place for far too long. Eventually the time comes for me to snap out of it, and of course I turn to my Father. My faith is what always pulls me back to the place of blessings. It's when we're in the middle of our difficulties and turn back to our faith that we rediscover the blessings that have been waiting for us all along. Is it time for you to let your faith pull you back to a place of blessing?

Lord, when I'm in a difficult place, please help me to keep coming back to you. Show me the way back, especially when I can't see it clearly. Amen

Mysteries

The "Mysterious Mountain" Symphony was written in 1955 by Hovhaness, who commented: "Mountains are symbols, like pyramids, of man's attempt to know God."

Psalm 73 TVT
Trying to solve this mystery on my own exhausted me;
I couldn't bear to look at it any further. So I took my questions
to the True God... I admit how broken I am
in body and spirit, but God is my strength,
and He will be mine forever.

The view out my kitchen window shows vistas of mountains and the grand peak of Mount Shasta in the distance. The shadows in between mountain ranges always intrigue me. Is it pure wilderness out there? Is there a road somewhere to explore those hills? I may never know, but I love the mystery. It seems that God gave a curious heart to each of us that draws us to the unknown. It makes me understand a little about why mountain climbers have to climb to the top, just to say they've done it.

There are other times when life's mysteries are not so interesting or intriguing. When life's troubles are weighing me down and I'm pressed to make hard decisions, it can be unbearable. I imagine everyone goes through anxious, trying times. It's part of the human condition, and if I didn't have my Father to turn to, I honestly don't know how I'd get through some of those difficult times. When I think about the people in the world who don't know Him, it truly saddens me to think of what a struggle life is without having the strength of the Lord to lean on. I love finding nuggets like the passage in Psalm 73 that tells me there is nothing unusual about what I'm going through, because someone thousands of years ago faced a similar dilemma and shared how they found the answers. They admitted how exhausted and broken they were and turned to God for their strength. The deeper we look into the Word of God, the more we find that the answers are always in there.

Thank you Father for giving us your precious words of guidance in the Bible. Thank you for the stories that show us we are not alone, that the troubles we have are not unique to us, and that you are always there to give us strength. Amen

Gold Mines

Refine: re•fine
remove impurities or unwanted elements

Proverbs 17:3 TPT
In the same way that gold and silver are
refined by fire, the Lord purifies your
heart by the tests and trials of life.

When I lived in Arizona, I bought a cabin near a remote, hundred year old mining town called Crown King. Half the adventure of spending time at the cabin was getting there - it was twenty eight miles of rough washboard dirt road to the town, and then another eight miles of an even rougher 4x4 road full of ruts and boulders to get to my cabin. In the town's hey day the town drew in people to try to "strike it rich" in gold mining. It seems that people are still trying to find the easy path to riches. A few may get lucky, but for the most part it takes hard work, and trying and failing a few times before you are successful at starting a business or climbing the ladder in a career.

In the same way, there is no instant way to become a godly, righteous person. It's a journey that may take a lifetime. Saying yes to Jesus is only the first step. God gives us opportunities to grow and learn by way of the tests and trials we have in life. It took me some years to figure this out, but I am finally getting it when the Bible says to "consider it pure joy when we face trials" (James 1:2), because God is building our character. Sure, I get frustrated by some of life's ups and downs, but I've learned to look for the lessons. Even if I can't quite define the lesson, I am learning to find peace in trusting that my Father has good plans for me, and is working everything out for my good, in spite of what I may be going through. Are you looking for the lessons in your difficult situation today?

Thank you, Lord, for purifying my heart and making me into a better person. Help me to see the lessons I need to learn so I can develop the character I need for the rest of the journey, and beyond. Amen

Moving Mountains

Earthquakes move mountains. *-Mitigation Works*

Psalm 46:2-3 TVT
No fear, no pacing, no biting fingernails. When the earth spins
out of control, we are sure and fearless. When mountains
crumble and the waters run wild, we are
sure and fearless. Even in heavy winds and huge waves, or as
mountains shake, we are sure and fearless.

The last couple years of living in a pandemic has felt like the world is spinning out of control for sure. It's been a crazy, wild ride with so many unexpected side effects of a tiny microscopic virus, that has left the whole world in a mess. Nothing will ever be the same. They say there's a "new normal," and all of us are trying to adjust. So much loss, so much heartache. How do we overcome this "spirit of fear" that has gripped the whole world?

The answer is to stand on our Rock, Jesus. This seems like such a simplistic statement, but most things with God are simple and profound like this. As the scripture above states, we are "sure and fearless" in the face of all the world issues when we have the Holy Spirit living inside us. We can know that no matter what is going on around us, we are secure in the Lord. Yes, there will be hardships and sickness in this life. I'm not saying we can get out of any of it. But there is a peace deep inside a believer's heart that can't be denied or explained. It is what gets us through even the chaos of a pandemic.

If fear is trying to get a grip on you, let it go right now. Give it to Jesus and stand on the Word that says we are "sure and fearless". Activate your faith; say it out loud, "I am sure and fearless", and lean into it. "God will never give you the spirit of fear, but the Holy Spirit gives you mighty power, love, and self-control." (2 Timothy 1:7 TPT)

Papa God, thank you for being my strength and my rock through the tragedies of life. Help me to keep coming back to that "sure and fearless" heart. Amen

Week Five Reflections and Journaling Points

Write your reflections of the readings from the last week.

<u>High on a Hill:</u> *What do you need to shake off today?*

<u>Mountain Pass:</u> *Coming back to God's place of blessing.*

<u>Mysteries:</u> *Find the answer to a problem in God's Word.*

<u>Gold Mines:</u> *How are you growing through tests & trials?*

<u>Moving Mountains:</u> *About letting go of a fear you have.*

<u>Other Reflections</u>

Mountains
Week Six

Restless Spirits

When I saw the mountains the weight lifted and my
restless spirit calmed...
I knew I was where I belong. *~Unknown*

Galations 4:6 TPT
And so that we would know for sure that we are his true
children, God released the Spirit of Sonship into our hearts,
moving us to cry out intimately, "My Father! You're our true
Father!"

I t's amazing how nature can bring us back to center when our spirits are out of sorts, and our minds are stressed. All our modern advancements and technologies have brought us many comforts in life, but there is nothing that can make us feel more at home like getting back to nature. For me, it's like some kind of deep inner feeling that we are connected to Earth in ways we can't explain.

In the same way, the Holy Spirit living within us is the thing that lifts our restless spirits to know in the depths of our hearts that God is our true Father. This was a real healing experience for me, because I never really had a loving father figure in my life. I remember the day the Holy Spirit set this knowledge into my heart. I was in a Vineyard Church service, and the pastor gave a word of knowledge that the Lord wanted to heal the hearts of the fatherless. All I had to do was receive it. Well, I knew that was for me, but there were many others touched that day as well. In that instant of surrender, I knew that God was my Father; has always been my Father, and he loves me just the way I am. He adopted me to be his own. I am not alone or unwanted. That revelation broke something in me. My hardened heart was healed that day. Oh how sweet it is when the Holy Spirit leads us to places of healing. What freedom there is when we lean into it! I encourage you to lean into those moments when you feel God speaking and asking you to release something to him. Don't hold back; let it go and be healed.

Thank you Holy Spirit for leading and guiding us on the paths of healing and into a deeper knowledge of your love. Amen

The Beauty of Nature

Nature is the art of God. ~*Dante*

Job 12:7-10 TVT
But ask the animals, and they will teach you, or the birds in the
sky, and they will tell you; or speak to the earth, and it will
teach you, or let the fish in the sea inform you. Which of all
these does not know that the hand of the Lord has done this? In
his hand is the life of every creature and the
breath of all mankind.

Our God is truly an artist. One of my favorite things to do is go exploring new places in nature. I love to drive to new destinations and spend time just gazing at more of God's beautiful creation. The southwest has the most spectacular landscapes I've ever seen. The red sands and monuments, the arches, and the magnificent Grand Canyon are truly inspiring. These kind of experiences live in our hearts and memories, and become a part of us. Things and people may come and go during our journey through life, but the beauty of nature and our time spent in it makes an impression on our soul that stays.

When was the last time you took some time out to marvel at creation and let it refresh your soul? I'm not talking about a vacation with every minute packed with activities and thrills like a theme park, but a quiet time away from everything where you can really still your spirit and rest. A time to see some natural beauty and soak it in, thanking Papa God for the wonderful creation that he has given to us. This is the essence of being still and knowing God. Speak to him and wait to hear his still small voice. "Blessed are those who listen to me, watching daily at my doors, waiting at my doorway. Those who find me find life and receive favor from the Lord." (Proverbs 8:34-35 NIV) Now that's my kind of R&R.

Father God, I stand amazed by the beauty you created in nature. Thank you for giving us richly, all things to enjoy. (1 Timothy 6:17) Amen

69

Challenging Trails

It's only after you've stepped outside your comfort zone
that you begin to change, grow, and transform.
~ *Roy T. Bennett*

Ephesians 2: 22 TPT
This means that God is transforming each one of you into the
Holy of Holies, his dwelling place, through the power of the
Holy Spirit living in you.

C ompleting a challenging mountain trail can change your life. I think it has something to do with facing and overcoming our fears, that really transforms us. I have several friends who have hiked to the bottom of the Grand Canyon and back, and they really do come back inspired and confident. I cannot hike the Canyon due to a foot ailment, so I opted for rafting through it, which proved to be just as challenging and thrilling for me. I believe it's the challenges in life that cause us to grow in character and self-esteem. I have personally found that pressing into a challenge, rather than shrinking back, is where the real growth happens.

The biggest transforming experience in my life was choosing to follow Jesus. I knew I needed him, but I really had no idea about the challenges ahead of me. I didn't realize I was signing up for the Holy Spirit to change me from the inside out to make me into his dwelling place. What a high honor! I'm sure if I knew this was the point, I might have shrunk back feeling like I was wholly inadequate for the job. In fact that kind of thinking kept me from surrendering to him for some time. But my need for him finally outweighed my insecurities about being good enough, and I stepped out in faith into the greatest adventure of my life. Since then the Lord has brought me through low valleys and over high mountaintops in the process of healing the innermost parts of me, which has been the "challenging" part. But the view from here (thirty nine years later) is beautiful and amazing. Are you pressing into your spiritual adventure, or shrinking back?

Thank you Father for giving me the boldness to press in when you are leading me through the mountaintops and the valleys of life. Amen

Pine Cones

The words of God are not like the oak leaf
which dies and falls to the earth, but like the
pine tree which stays green forever.
-*Mohawk Wisdom*

Proverbs 27:9 NIV
Perfume and incense bring joy to the heart,
and the pleasantness of a friend springs
from their heartfelt advice.

Have you ever looked closely at a fresh pine cone? There are many styles and shapes, and a short study in my own back yard has amazed me at their diversity and beauty. The fir trees, which look like your typical Christmas tree, actually have small pine cones with paper thin petals, yet their colors and patterns match the giant pine cone petals from the sugar pine tree. Some pine cones are smooth and others are prickly! The ponderosa pine have the typical pine cones we think of in shape and size, and they are abundant around my property. They seem too beautiful to just rake up and throw away, so I started researching the many uses for them and got creative. There are a lot of ways to use pine cones.

The same could be said of how we use our words. Sometimes they are caring and bring encouragement to others, and other times our words are hurtful and prickly. It seems I'm constantly trying to figure out how to be more gracious and loving with my words. How I wish all my words were as beautiful as a fresh pine cone. I have pine cones around my house, and when I need to get control of my words, I can pick one up and turn it in my fingers to help give me pause in the conversation. I feel the prickly points and remember not to speak that way to those I love. Maybe a pine cone around your house can help you from being too prickly with your words too.

Papa God, continue to help me with my words. Continue to show me the life lessons I need to speak heartfelt advice to those who hear me, and may I more often than not, speak out of love. Amen

Mountaintop Moments

At some moments we experience complete unity within
us and around us. This may happen when we stand on a
mountaintop and are captivated by the view.
~*Henri Nouwen*

Matthew 14:23 TVT
After He had sent them away, He went up the mountain by Himself to pray. When evening came, He was there alone.

Mountaintops are physically hard places to get to. Maybe that's why they have such a special effect on us. We know that so few have been there, and it ignites something inside us that makes us feel whole when we experience that unmistakably unique moment in our life that may never come again. This must be what drives mountain climbers to conquer the mountain tops of the world.

Jesus made a habit of going to the mountain tops to get alone and pray during the peak of his ministry. It's something we can learn to do, to strengthen our ministry and our own walk with God. I'm not a big hiker, but I do love to drive to the mountains to be inspired and get some alone time with God. If it was good for Jesus, it's got to be good for me!

Another way we experience mountaintop experiences is on the inside, in our spirits. It's those moments in life that bring great rejoicing, and during those moments we feel on top of the world; your first job, your wedding day, completing a long hard project, the day you said yes to Jesus. We would love for every day to have high moments, but real life is not like that. When the road leads us to the valleys, that's when we can recall the mountaintops and know this is only temporary. We can push through and look for that next day of rejoicing. If you find yourself stuck in a valley, don't stay there. Get up, get out and go find a mountaintop! Ask the Lord to meet you there, and lean into his presence. You'll come back a different person.

Thank you Jesus for your example of getting away to the mountains to be alone with our Father. Thank you for meeting us there and giving us strength. Amen

Week Six Reflections and Journaling Points

Write your reflections of the readings from the last week.

<u>Restless Spirit:</u> *Lean in and release something to God.*

<u>Beauty of Nature:</u> *Be still and listen-what is God saying to you.*

<u>Challenging Trails:</u> *Pressing in to your spiritual adventure.*

<u>Pine Cones:</u> *Haw can we be more gracious with your words?*

<u>Mountain Top Moments:</u> *Write about a mountain top moment.*

<u>Other Reflections</u>

Waters
NATURE'S HEALING THERAPY

Introduction

Thousands have lived without love, not one
has lived without water. - *H. Auden*

"...and the Spirit of God was hovering over the waters." Genesis 1:2 NIV

I find pure delight in nature and things created. My favorite places to travel always involve exploring more of nature. My husband and I have been on many road trips around the good old USA from one coast to the other. We have visited many State and National Parks, but I have to say, most of the beautiful places on planet Earth have something to do with water. Camping and hiking by the rivers, creeks, lakes and water falls always bring a sense of peace and healing to my soul.

"He makes me lie down in green pastures, He leads me beside quiet waters. He refreshes my soul, and guides me along the right paths..." *Psalm 23*

I hope these pages bring you a sense of peace to start your day, and healing for your body and soul to take you into the future. Just a few moments each day spent with focus on seeking the Lord through his word and his creation, can work miracles. Listen for the Lord to speak to you through the scriptures and lean in to where he might lead. I hope you take the time to journal every five days to write down your thoughts. I have found that journalling helps me to let go of anxieties, and embrace the promises God has for me. He has so much to teach us through his creation!

May the Lord bless you through this journey. ~Linda

Waters
Week One

A Joyful Song

May what I do flow from me like a river, no forcing and no
holding back, the way it is with children.
~Rainer Maria Rilke

Psalm 98:8 NIV
Let the rivers applaud and the
mountains join in joyful song...

I love to have quiet moments of meditation in nature. Just listening to the sounds of the forest or a gurgling creek can be so soothing. If you listen carefully to the sound of a trickling water fall, you can hear the music it makes. It's like a joyful laughing song.

One day in late Spring my husband and I were having our morning devotions out on our deck. There was a quiet moment of listening to the wind in the trees... a bird here - and over there. The woosh, woosh, woosh of a big birds' wings as it flew overhead. The trees were swaying in the breeze, like they were dancing to the music of the wind. It made me want to sing my own song to the Lord, and so I did. Then my husband began playing his wooden flute; a sweet sultry sound as a love song to our Jesus. There is something so freeing about true worship and praise to our God... it moves our spirits to a place of opening up and letting the Spirit of the Living God come in. His loving, healing Spirit. It's so good.

Go ahead and sing a new song to the Lord. Sing *your* song to the Lord. Feel the freedom, the love and the healing coming back as the God of creation hears you and communes with your spirit in the midst of it.

My Jesus, my Lord, you are so worthy to be praised in spirit and in truth. Thank you for the gift of music and song that gives us a way for our hearts to touch yours. Amen

Morning Fog

If you want to see what the fog hides in itself, don't wait
for the fog to disperse! Instead of waiting for something
to happen in this short life, do something immediately!
Enter the fog! ~ *Mehmet Murat ildan*

Nehemiah 2 TVT
...I prayed to the God of heaven and made my request... My True God had heard my prayers and rested His hand of favor and love upon me.

S ome mornings the view out my window shows sun on the mountain and dense fog down in the valley. It feels like I've got an advantage being up on the ridge. I can see clearly, but the people living down in the valley are in the fog, and it won't be clearing up for them for a while.

Life is like that sometimes. When things are weighing us down, or we feel lost and we don't have answers, it's like living in a fog. Sometimes it takes me a while, but I know the thing to do in these situations is to seek the Lord. He's the only one with the real answers. I can't keep living in the fog of indecision. Eventually I need to do something to find my way out, even if it means stepping out in blind faith. If I've said all my prayers, and asked for all my needs, all I can do is act, and believe the Lord will guide my steps and give me favor. The bible tells me that when I find myself in trying times, he will provide a way out. (See 1 Cor 10:13) When we believe in that, we've already won.

Thank you Father for being there every time I need you. Thank you for hearing me and guiding me when I'm lost in a fog. Amen

Morning Rains

There is something magical about the early morning. It's a time when the world belongs to only those few who are awake. And we walk around like kings while others remain unseen in their beds. *~Shawn Blanc*

2 Samuel 23:3-5 TVT
...The one who leads people with justice and in the fear of God
is like the morning light; the sun rising on a cloudless morning,
and the shining grasslands
brought up from rain.

I like getting up early. It's hard for me to sleep past 7am most days. I count it a blessing to catch a sunrise as I'm starting my day. A sunrise feels like something special, one of those things that not everyone gets to see. I's like I just witnessed a once in a lifetime event that is unique to me and my perspective from where I am standing in the world, in that one moment in time. Early mornings can be even more beautiful if they follow a good rain and everything is fresh & clean with the morning sun shining on it. The pine trees are sparkling with water drops on each little needle.

Isn't it amazing to think about how we are like that first "morning light, rising on a cloudless morning" to the Lord? When we represent him well, when we are leaders in his Kingdom sharing our faith, when we are being shining lights to give others a glimpse of our Jesus, we are like the morning sun light. I like that picture. It inspires me to shine a little brighter. I think the reason God gives us these kinds of visions, is because he knows we are visual people. He inspires us with beautiful word-pictures to communicate his thoughts to us.

Father, you are an artist bringing beautiful pictures to our minds. Thank you Lord for how you communicate to show us what we look like to you. Open my mind to see more. Amen

The Scent of Rain

One of my favorite words: Petrichor - the smell in the air
around the time when rain falls on dry, stony ground.
~Carol Gardner.   Etymology from Greek: petros =
"stone"; ichor = "divine fluid, the blood of the gods

Through our yielded lives he spreads the fragrance of the knowledge of God everywhere we go. We become the unmistakable aroma of the victory of the Anointed One to God - a perfume of life to those being saved...

I love being in a mountain forest, and smelling the pine fragrance in the air; or sitting on a front porch just before it rains. Nature has some pure and distinct smells. They aren't like other smells that remind you of something, like they way your Mom made chocolate chip cookies. The smells of nature have a unique way of touching us that connects us to planet Earth. For me, it brings me back to the basic notion that we are all part of God's creation.

Through God's grace and the deposit of the Holy Spirit we've been given, many of us recognize him, but there are so many more that don't. It is a strange invisible thing, faith, that divides people into two completely different walks of life. When I'm around believers, there is almost an instant kindred spirit of love that connects us. But when I'm around unbelievers, an unusual thing happens... they will act differently. They might totally reject me out of their own convictions, or they will go the opposite way; becoming gentler and apologizing for bad language.

Is it me they show this special disdain or respect for? No, I think it's the Spirit of the Lord inside me that they recognize. Like the scripture above says, we have the unmistakable aroma of Jesus. All we have to do is live our lives yielded to him, and he uses us to spread the knowledge of God like the distinct fragrance of our Creator. What kind of perfume are you wearing today?

Lord help me to live my life in a way that allows your beautiful fragrance to spread the knowledge of your Son everywhere I go. Amen

The Right Path

Sometimes the right path is not the easiest.
~Grandmother Willow

Isaiah 40:27-28 TVT
Why do you say, "My troubled path is hidden from the Eternal;
God has lost all interest in my cause."? Don't you know?
Haven't you heard? The Eternal, the Everlasting God, The
Creator of the whole world, never gets tired or weary. His
wisdom is beyond understanding.

There is something special about water in nature. Spending time at a river, stream or lake is like a day of therapy. It calms the mind and refreshes the spirit. When I was a young girl, we would always go camping by our favorite lake. And as a teenager, I spent every weekend I could at the beach. Basically water has always been one of my favorite places to go to get some fun, refreshing and inner healing.

Sometimes the path of life takes us places we never intended to go, and it's in those times, that my favorite places are exactly where I want to go for a time out. I know everyone has hard times. It almost seems inevitable that we will all go through some rough times. I think it's a part of life that is there with the purpose to help us learn and grow.

The scripture today reminds me that others go through the same troubling times and feel like I do - asking God, "where are you?" And then God comes back with an almost sarcastic answer; "Have you forgotten who I am?" Well, that requires an attitude adjustment on my part! So when I get over my pity party and speak to my Father from a sincere heart, that's when the breakthrough happens, and I get back on the right path. He strengthens me in my weariness, and brings back my vitality. And maybe I am a little wiser for the worst of it. Do you need an attitude adjustment toward your Father today?

Papa God, thank you for always being there for me to turn to in the hard times. Help me to learn how to get through them with you (not without you). Help me to learn the lessons I need to learn. Amen

Waters Week One Reflections and Journaling Points

Write your reflections of the readings from the last week.

A Joyful Song: Sing a new song to the Lord.

Morning Fog: Ask the Lord to clear up an issue of indecision.

Morning Rain: Write about a word-picture the Lord gave you.

Scent of Rain: How do you spread the fragrance of Jesus?

The Right Path: How God strengthens you in your weariness.

Other Reflections

Waters
Week Two

Cool Waters

Good news is rare these days and every glittering
ounce of it should be cherished and hoarded and
worshipped and fondled like a priceless diamond.
~Hunter S Thompson

Proverbs 25:25 TVT
Like cool water to a weary soul, so is good news
from a distant country.

I had the awesome experience of rafting down the Colorado River through the Grand Canyon many years ago. It was a five day trip, and we camped along the way on narrow landings along the river, and slept under the stars. It was so hot in the canyon during the day, we took opportunities to dip into the river every chance we got. One morning we got some great news about making a special stop. We pulled into a cove and hiked down a side canyon to a beautiful waterfall and pool. It's the one and only time in my life that I got to stand under the cool spray of a waterfall. If this is not on your bucket list, it should be. It was exhilarating.

Wouldn't it be nice if we could share more good news and happy surprises with each other? In today's world of constant bad news and living through a pandemic, a little good news can go a long way. When it feels like there's no good news to share, we need to be creative and think of ways to bring a little joy and a few smiles to the people in our circle of influence. The Bible says, "whatever is true, whatever is noble, whatever is right, whatever is pure, whatever is lovely, whatever is admirable; if anything is excellent or praiseworthy, think about such things; and the God of Peace will be with you." (Phil 4:8-9) Let's not focus on the bad news any more. Let's be part of what is good and right in the world. Is there someone you know who needs to hear some good news today?

Father I would love to be the bearer of good news for someone today. Show me who. Show me how. Amen.

Spring Wells

"We never know the worth of water till the well is dry."
- *Thomas Fuller*

John 4:14 NIV
...but whoever drinks the water I give them will never thirst. Indeed, the water I give them will become in them a spring of water welling up to eternal life.

It was the day before Thanksgiving, and we were expecting family. Not just from out of town, but visiting from another country. Unbelievably, just two hours before their arrival, our spring well ran dry. I was devastated, and it was a fiasco getting through the holiday without water. We had a storage tank, but being a holiday weekend, we couldn't find anyone to deliver water way out in our neck of the woods. The best we could do was drive into town and buy as much bottled water as we could find. But there was no running water, no showers, and this mama was just a tad bit flustered!

Imagine the days when women had to go to the well every day to get water for their household. We've certainly been spoiled with the luxuries of modern technologies. This "dry well" experience really brings home the symbolic meaning of the bible verse today. The Spirit of the living God in us is like a spring of water welling up into eternal life. We will never "run dry" and die like my water well did. We have the promise of eternity planted in our hearts. That surety is what makes all the troubles of life seem trivial. 2nd Corinthians chapter 4 says, "our momentary troubles are achieving for us an eternal glory that far out weights them all. So we fix our eyes not on what is seen, but on what is unseen, since what is seen is temporary, but what is unseen is eternal." So when these little tests and trials come into our lives, let's try to remember this is only temporary, and that we are like aliens living in a foreign land. Someday we will go home.

Thank you Lord for your Spirit inside me that tells me everything will be ok. Forgive my momentary insanity when things don't go as planned. Thank you for always bringing me back to the truth about what really matters. Amen

Mighty Waters

Water is the driving force of all nature.
~*Leonardo da Vinci*

Job 12:13 TVT
But true wisdom and power are found in God;
counsel and understanding are His.

My husband and I took an RV vacation some years ago, and visited several national parks. Niagara Falls was one of the most impressive places we visited. When you arrive at the park, it's shocking to find out it's in the middle of a big city! You walk along a sidewalk by a river with a quiet, but strong current, to the edge of a cliff to see the water plummeting down in a spectacular raging symphony that is beautiful and dangerous and powerful.

It is really amazing to think about the way water represents both life and death on planet Earth. Without it nothing could survive, but it also has a destructive power that can't be rivaled. I think the same could be said about our Creator. He is the life giving source, and without him, there is death.

Some of these deep truths are hard to ponder and understand, but there is no denying that our God, the Creator of the universe, is all powerful, all mighty, all knowing and always present. It makes one feel very humble before a Holy God. Who are we that he is mindful of us? And yet we are his prized possession, his masterpiece, and he loves us with an everlasting love. He bestows upon us his grace, his wisdom, counsel and understanding. He sends his son to die for us, and puts his Spirit into us so that he can call us his own.. and so we can call him, Papa God.

I love You Lord - my Father, my Jesus, my precious Holy Spirit. I am humbled in your presence and by your extravagant love. Thank you for seeing me, understanding me, and adopting me. Amen

Pouring Rain

Only a select few are able to see the true beauty that lies behind what just might seem like a rainy day or a grey sky. ~*Jessica Laar*

Joel 2:28-29 TVT

In those days I will pour my Spirit to all humanity; your children will boldly and prophetically speak the word of God. Your elders will dream dreams; your young men will see visions. No one will be left out. In those days I will offer my Spirit to all...

The rains can be a welcome sight after a long drought. We had a drought that had gone on for 3 years in my area, and the entire forest was bone dry. Prayers for rain were a daily thing. I found myself amazed at how the forest could survive all those months without a drop of water. Then finally, some rain. Not just a little rain... pouring rain for days and days, until I started to wonder when it was going to stop. The ground was so saturated that there was standing water everywhere, rivers and creeks were all swollen. Thank you Lord!

God has a different kind of outpouring that also changes things on planet Earth, on a spiritual level. At a time when there was a spiritual drought, our Father poured his Spirit out upon all mankind through his son Jesus. After making the supreme sacrifice for all of us, he sent the Holy Spirit, our comforter, our helper, and the bearer of gifts. God's Spirit is the giver of of life, grace, prophecy, truth, healing and holiness. He teaches and directs us on the right paths to follow. He intercedes for us and guides our prayers, He empowers us and gives us wisdom and understanding when we need it. The same Spirit that raised Christ from the dead, lives in us! It sort of boggles the mind, doesn't it? That much power in us? Imagine what we could accomplish for the Kingdom if we all embraced these gifts and allowed them to work in us. Now is not the time to shrink back because we feel inadequate. The gifts will empower us when we boldly step into them. Let us be people who say "Here am I, use me."

Thank you Father for the amazing privilege of serving you through the gifts of your Holy Spirit. My hands are open to receive. Pour hour Spirit out! Amen

Deep Waters

This world is in deep trouble, from top to bottom.
But it can be swiftly healed by the balm of love."
~Rumi quotes from Quotefancy.com

2 Samuel 22:17-18 NIV
"He reached down from on high and took hold of me; he drew me out of deep waters. He rescued me from my powerful enemy, from my foes, who were too strong for me.

Have you ever felt like you were over your head in a troubling situation? Maybe you bit off more than you can actually chew, or took on more than you should have, and now the stress is overwhelming. Or maybe your trouble has to do with having bad people in your life that can potentially cause you big problems.

I have learned a couple things over the years that maybe you can glean from so it doesn't take you as long as it did me to detangle my life from these life stresses. First, learn to say no (in a loving way) so you don't over commit. Second, weed out the people in your life that pull you in the wrong direction. This is the hard part, as we love our friends. I took a radical approach to this when I was in my twenties, by moving to another state to get away from the crazy lifestyle I was in. This isn't always the best solution for everyone, but it worked for me. I got a clean 'do-over' that got me on the right track.

What ever your deep trouble is, the Lord can pull you out. I know that is not the first thought that comes to mind when we are in that stressful place, but I found the scripture for you. Use this scripture gem to speak the answer into your situation, by personalizing it:

Father, please reach down from heaven and take hold of me in this stressful situation. Draw me out of these deep waters. Rescue me from my enemies (which is sometimes myself when I overcommit). Give me wisdom to see the way out, or the way to finish strong. Amen

Waters Week Two Reflection and Journaling Points

Write your reflections of the readings from the last week.

<u>Cool Waters:</u> *What good news have you shared lately?*

<u>Spring Wells:</u> *What temporary trouble can you give to God?*

<u>Mighty Waters:</u> *How does God love you extravagantly?*

<u>Pouring Rain:</u> *write a prayer to release the Holy Spirit over you.*

<u>Deep Waters:</u> *How can God help you out of deep troubles?*

<u>Other Reflections</u>

Waters
Week Three

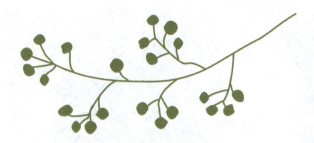

Wellspring of Life

Nothing is softer or more flexible than water,
yet nothing can resist it. ~ *Lao*

John 4:14 TVT
I offer water that will become a wellspring within
you that gives life throughout eternity. You will
never be thirsty again.

Water in all its forms is always a thing a beauty. Whether it's a trickling stream, pure white snow, or an ocean. It can bring peace just sitting by quiet waters, and yet it can dissolve a rock, given enough time. It's not surprising that Jesus used the power of life giving water to illustrate how the Spirit within us is like a wellspring of water flowing into eternity.

It reminds me about a time when my daughter and I went floating down the Shenandoah river on floaties. There was very little effort needed, because the current of the water easily took us along its path. It was all fun, until we ran aground and had to walk on the slippery rocks to the deeper part of the stream to keep going again. Riding along back in the flow, we were having quite a good time, until we came across a section filled with tiny beetles. We were being covered in little water bugs, which really freaked us out. We got out and away from that section with a few screams and skirmishes! A little further along, we were back to enjoying the water.

Does it seem like our spiritual journey is sometimes like that? We're going happily along, rejoicing in our Jesus, when obstacles get in our way and we get sidetracked. Or a badgering problem distracts us and we step off the path momentarily. These little tests will teach us life lessons and build character, but the biggest thing we are learning is how to reconnect with the Spirit of God, and get back into the flow of the wellspring within us. Do you need to redirect or get back into the flow today?

Papa God, thank you for always being there to draw me home when the ways of the world and the plans of the enemy are distracting me from what is important. Help me to never take my eyes off you. Amen

Reflections

Water is a reflective surface. When the water in a lake or sea is very still, the reflection of the landscape is perfect, because the reflecting surface is very flat. However, if there are ripples or waves in the water, the reflection becomes distorted. *~Sciencelearn.org*

Proverbs 1:23 TPT
Don't you know that I'm ready to pour out my Spirit of Wisdom upon you and bring to you the revelation of my words that will make your heart wise?

Our lives should be a reflection of Gods goodness in the world, but it's sometimes hard to reflect a perfect God, when our lives are full of ripples and distortions, right? It's always my prayer that people will see God in me, but when I'm having a bad day, I hope no one is looking. It's like Paul says, I do what I don't want to do, and I blow up my testimony before others. It truly saddens me when that happens!

The first chapter of Proverbs is a very thought provoking passage on the subject, and a sad commentary of what happens when we ignore God and go our own way. "Don't you know I'm ready to pour out my Spirit of Wisdom upon you?" He asks. He talks to the foolish hearts and offers us wisdom, saying it's right in front of us - in the hustle and bustle of everyday life. He's ready to give me "the revelation of His Word to make my heart wise", and who wouldn't want that? Wisdom of the heart is different than wisdom in your mind. Treasures are waiting for those of us that listen to him. Peace, freedom from fear, confidence, courage and resting unafraid from the storms of life. All heart issues. (See verse 33.) These promises are what anchors my faith, along with a bit (or quite a lot) of His grace that forgives me when I stumble around in life.

Papa God, please keep pouring out your Spirit of Wisdom on me! Give me more revelation of your words, and make my heart wise. Amen

Watery Beginnings

It's a substance that covers around 71% of Earth's surface and one that is needed, to varying degrees, by nearly all living organisms. Despite its importance and prevalence, science is still trying to nail down the specifics of how, when, and from where Earth's water originated.

~Weatherology.com

Proverbs 3:19-20 TPT
The Lord laid the earth's foundations with wisdom's blueprints.
By his living-understanding all the universe came into being.
By his divine revelation he broke open the hidden fountains of
the deep, bringing secret springs to the surface as the mist of
the night dripped down from heaven.

When astronomers look for life out in the universe, they are always on the lookout for a sign of water, as if it was the source of life. On planet Earth, it's true that all life depends on water. Our Creator designed it that way. If the scientists want to know where the water came from, they should read the scripture here. Now I know that the world at large will push away these ideas as foolishness (1 Cor 1:13), but it still tends to frustrate me that people don't understand the simple truth about a Creator. They tediously search for something else to explain the origins of life.

I have a family member that is basically atheistic. His work is teaching others about nature from a purely evolutionary perspective. We have had debates and I've bought books and videos for him that I thought might enlighten him, but it only pushed him away. I miss him in my life. He has a wonderful adventurous spirit that I love. I still pray the Lord will one day open his eyes. I hope he knows I love him.

Sometimes our faith does come between us and our family and friends, and it can be painful. But Jesus teaches us that this is to be expected (see Luke 12:51-52). Our lives in Christ are to be so appealing that others will want what we have. But there are many that have hardened hearts. I believe our prayers can move God to soften those hearts. Let's not forget to keep those we love, that don't know the Lord, in our prayers.

Papa God, I ask for you to heal the hearts of those separated from loved ones, and open the eyes of those that are blind. Show us both the way of love. Amen

Fountain of Life

Be like the fountain that overflows, not like the cistern that merely contains. ~*Paulo Coelho*

Proverbs 8:35 TPT
For the fountain of life pours into you every time that you find me, and this is the secret of growing in the delight and the favor of the Lord.

When I was in high school, I loved art class. The teacher was my all time favorite, and not just because I loved art, but because she believed in me. This teacher inspired me and encouraged me to let my creative juices flow. She was so kind and really poured into me at a time when life at home was really tough. Maybe she sensed that I was a troubled teen, and needed a little love. People like that make a lasting impression. I thank God for her. I hope I can be that person to others that need encouragement in a trying time of life.

The passage today has become another strong influence that lifts me up when life is dragging me down. In those moments we can find ourselves succumbing to emotions and losing our peace. Hopefully before we go to too far down that road, we come around and reach out to the Lord, because we know he can give us the power we need to overcome. When we find God in these circumstances, his fountain of life fills us up again. Not only do we get our peace back, but he is delighted in us! We gain his favor, and we grow in our faith. Sounds like a win-win to me. I love the idea of my Father being delighted with me, the same way my art teacher was, except he is seeing me at my worst. What a loving Father we have. And what is really cool, is that we can pay it forward. Is there someone that you could pour a little love into today?

Papa God, thank you for always being there when I am hurting and reminding me that I'm never alone. Thank you for pouring your life giving Spirit into me and showing me the secrets of growing in your delight and favor. Show me how to pay it forward. I love you Lord. Amen

Mountain Springs

There is a fountain of youth: it is your mind, your talents, the creativity you bring to your life and the lives of people you love. ~ *Sophia Loren*

Proverbs 16:22 TPT
Wisdom is a deep well of understanding opened up within you as a fountain of life for others...

Living in the forest where city water isn't available for miles around, I've learned a lot about how planet Earth works in storing water underground. I'm so thankful that God made it this way, so people could populate the remote and beautiful places in the world. At the bottom of the steep hill on our property, there is a natural spring that flows from the deep parts of the mountain - what a blessing to have the natural spring water as our water source!

The scripture today portrays wisdom as a "deep well of understanding", which reminds me of a mountain spring. But the point that sticks out to me in this passage is that the wisdom is poured out from deep within us, flowing as a fountain of life to others. Isn't that a beautiful picture? Just like the water in my spring makes life possible at my house (trust me, life stops when the water stops flowing), wisdom that flows out to others, brings life to them. What an honor, that our lives could be used this way. Sometimes we struggle so much with our own life, we forget that we are designed to be a conduit of life to others. If we take our eyes off ourselves long enough, we can really make a difference in the world.

To have wisdom flowing out of us, we need to fill up on it, and God's word. The book of Proverbs is a storehouse of wisdom waiting to be absorbed. I encourage you to fill up, and let it flow through. Look for someone you can add a little life to today.

Thank you Father for mountain springs, and wisdom from your Word that flows through me to others. Lord fill me up deep inside, so it overflows to those around me, bringing your love and life to their deep dry places. Amen

Waters Week Three Reflection and Journaling Points

Write your reflections of the readings from the last week.

<u>*WellSpring:*</u> *What life lessons are you learning from trials?*

<u>*Reflections:*</u> *Write about treasures of the heart God has given.*

<u>*Watery Beginnings:*</u> *Pray the Lord will soften a hard heart.*

<u>*Fountain of Life:*</u> *Think of a blessing you can pay forward.*

<u>*Mountain Springs:*</u> *What wisdom can you let flow to others?*

<u>*Other Reflections:*</u>

Waters
Week Four

Fresh Flowing Brook

Fresh water falls as a mist, rain or snow. ~*Wikipedia*

Proverbs 18:4 TPT
Words of wisdom are like a fresh, flowing brook - like deep
waters that spring forth from within, bubbling up
inside the one with understanding.

Here is yet another reference to how wisdom comes up from deep within us, flowing out. It must be an important issue the Lord wants us to learn. He gives us this beautiful flowing water word picture to help us get it. How do we access the deep spring inside us? With understanding. And how do we get the understanding? It all sounds like such a mystery, doesn't it? But true to the genius of our Lord, it's something very simple and profound. Our understanding comes from the Holy Spirit inside of us. Deep inside. Those of us who have received the promise of the precious Holy Spirit from the Lord Jesus, know things. Things that can only be known by faith. Yes, we are a special people. A chosen generation. A royal priesthood, called out of darkness into his marvelous light. (1 Peter 2:9)

As a gardener, I can help my plants grow to their best and biggest, by watering with fertilizers on a regular basis. But there is nothing my garden loves more than what I call "God Water". Rain falling from the sky. The fresh water from the clouds make everything in my garden visibly happier and healthier. It's another picture of how we effect the world when our wisdom and understanding flows out from those deep places in our heart. It's like we are sending "God Rain" to the world around us, and we leave it visibly better. It's our calling as children of the Most High God. Maybe you don't feel like a royal priest bestowing wisdom upon the world today, but that is how God sees us. How about digging deep for some words of wisdom that will leave the world visibly better today? All we have to do is let it bubble up and flow.

Papa God, I am amazed at how you see us and have set us apart to do a special work in the Earth. Help us to step into our role as your royal priesthood. Amen

Snow Fall

When snow falls, nature listens. *~ Antoinette Van Kleeff*

Job 37:5-7
He says to the snow, "Fall on the Earth", and to the
rain shower, "Be a mighty downpour."

There is something special about being in a gentle falling snow storm. Everything is still and quiet, and the earth is blanketed in clean crisp white. It somehow feels cleansing. That is, until the next day, when you realize that gentle snowfall left 3 feet of powder to dig through to get out of the driveway! One year it was especially (not) fun when we would dig out to the driveway, and a snowplow would come by and pile up snow and ice so thick it took a pick ax to get through it, then overnight another plow piled it all up again! But snow is beautiful... and cold. My husband says "the best place to enjoy snow is inside by the fireplace."

There is some interesting science about why the world gets so quiet in a snow storm, and for up to 24 hours afterwards. Snow actually absorbs sound when it's fluffy, according to the Michigan State University Extension. I personally believe that God designed it this way so the experience of snow would bless the world with a little peace and quiet. A momentary respite from the noise of life. There is a sovereign quality about quietness. The bible mentions it many times with "peace" in the same sentence. In quietness is where we hear the still small voice of God. In quietness and trust is our strength. Jesus called the disciples to come away with him to a quiet place to get some rest. Paul also taught that we should make it our ambition to lead a quiet life. Is your life needing some quiet time to listen for God and take a rest with peace and quiet? The world moves at a fast pace, so we need to make it a priority to "be still" once in a while.

Papa God, sometimes I just want some quiet time to curl up in your lap and soak up what you have to say to me. Help me to find ways to have quiet time with you. Amen

The Sound of Water

Many people swear watery sounds help them fall asleep... These slow, whooshing noises are the sounds of non-threats, which is why they work to calm people. It's like they're saying: "Don't worry, don't worry, don't worry." ~ *Livescience.com*

Proverbs 23:19 TPT
As you listen to me, my beloved child, you will grow in wisdom and your heart will be drawn into understanding, which will empower you to make right decisions.

In the summer time it is blazing hot in my neck of the woods. My husband & I found a nearby creek with a small swimming hole, that is a nice place to take a break from work to cool off. I like to pack a lunch and sit in the shade trees after we've cooled off, and just listen to the water running over the rocks as we eat. I can't tell which is the better therapy... the cool water, or just sitting by the sound of water. It is truly relaxing, and helps me to get back to work feeling refreshed and empowered to complete the work day.

Another way we are empowered, is by listening to God, which is mainly his written Word, the Bible, although there is also that "Still small voice". Proverbs 23 offers a powerful promise and insight about how to grow in wisdom to make right decisions. Like most of the promises God gives us, they generally aren't an instant solution. It takes time, sometimes a lifetime, to absorb what the Bible has to say to us. It's not the kind of book you can read from cover to cover once and be done. The miraculous thing about this book, is that the same passages can speak completely different sentiments to many different people. It's very personal to every person, like a spoken word from God just for us personally. Of course to get that personal interpretation, we need the Holy Spirit to translate for us. Those that don't have the Spirit on the inside, tend to see the scriptures as foolishness. Aren't you glad we have that very special gift?

Holy Spirit, I am unspeakably grateful for your inspiration and wisdom in revealing the scripture's personal message to me. What an amazing blessing. Help me to keep listening and growing. Amen

Water of Life

Water is such an essential component of life, it was created on the very first day. ~ *Duke University Blog*

Genesis 1:2 NIV
The Earth was a formless void and darkenss covered the face of the deep, while a wind from God swept over the face of the waters.

Have you ever seen the movie Water World? It's about a futuristic planet Earth, where the world is covered with water. I can imagine this might be what it was like in the passage today from Genesis; formless and void. No mountains or valleys, just the wind blowing over the face of the waters on the first day of creation. In Revelation chapter 22, it says, "The Spirit and the bride say, Come. And let everyone who is thirsty come. Let anyone who wishes, take the water of life as a gift." So from the beginning, right to the end, water gives life. First it gives life to planet Earth in physical form, then we are offered the "water of life" in a spiritual form to live forever. This is the water Jesus mentions to the woman at the well. That whoever drinks His water will never thirst again.

We can't begin to imagine what it will be like to step into eternity, but by faith, we know it's there. We get glimpses of it in the Bible, but it also says that no mind can imagine what the Lord is preparing for us. Jesus told the man on the cross beside him that today he would be in "paradise". That sounds pretty good to me! Even though we know it's there, we also tend to cling to this life, and pray for loved ones to get more time here during a deathly illness. Maybe it's a little selfish because really, we just want more time with them. But knowing this life is not the end, is what gives us peace of mind, and why we can say "it is well with my soul". Let go of the little things that bother you today, and just think about how this life is but a breath, and then it's gone. But we have paradise to look forward to. Enjoy each day on Earth we are given.

Thank you Father for that inner peace to know we will get to meet you face to face one day. It is well with my soul, Amen

Thunderstorms

They say marriages are made in Heaven. But so is
thunder and lightning. ~*Clint Eastwood*

Proverbs 25:23 TPT
As the north wind brings a storm, saying things you shouldn't
brings a storm to any relationship.

I remember a road trip I took in my youth with my best girlfriend at the time, to Lubbock Texas from southern California. We got caught in one bugger of a thunderstorm out in the middle of no where. We had to keep driving to the closest town to get to some safe shelter. It was the most horrendous scary storm I have ever been caught out in. The deluge of water coming out of the sky was unbelievable. We stopped at a gas station, parked by the pumps, and got soaked from head to toe just running 20 feet into the store! I'm sure flash floods and mud slide damage followed in the wake of that storm.

The internal storms we go through can be just as horrific and damaging as the watery kind. Sadly, most of those kind of storms are due to our words, just like the proverb above describes. To some degree, everyone needs to learn how to control our tongues, and I admit I am a prime example. It does hurt to go through an emotional storm, and it can hurt even more, when our own words have caused the storm in someone else's life unintentionally. Both scenarios require forgiveness and grace to get through. Sometimes the healing takes a lot of time as well. I know we all have our lessons to learn, but my heart hopes that because you're reading this, you can catch the spirit of what I'm sharing, and skirt around these kinds of tragedies without having to experience the hard lessons. Let me encourage you to do everything in love. Keep your words sweet and life giving. Be quick to forgive others and yourself.

Papa God, thank you for healing our hearts of these hurts, and teaching us how to be a better person. Amen

Waters Week Four Reflections and Journaling Points

Write your reflections of the readings from the last week.

Fresh Flowing Brook: *Write down - I am a royal priest.*

Snowfall: *How can you seek peace and quiet this week?*

Sound of Water: *What has God's Spirit spoken to you?*

Water of Life: *How can you enjoy each day on planet Earth?*

Thunder Storms: *How can God help you tame your tongue?*

Other Reflections

Waters
Week Five

Love Flows Like Water

Love is like water. We can fall in it. We can drown in it.
And we can't live without it. ~*PureLoveQuotes.com*

Song of Solomon 4:15 TPT
Your life flows into mine, pure as a garden spring. A well of living water springs up from within you like a mountain brook flowing into my heart!

I have to love how passionate Solomon was in his writings. He really had some good lines. The scripture today was a song or poem written to his lover, and talks about pure love (water) flowing from her heart to his, like a mountain brook. It makes me sigh just thinking about that kind of love. If you think about these words coming from our Father to his children, it takes on a whole new feeling. My eyes well up imagining a Father's love like that. A love I regret that I never knew growing up. But God is good, and he sent His Spirit to fill that hole in my heart with himself. The day I said yes to Jesus, the water (his love) started to flow into my heart. Then the day he asked me to let him heal my fatherless heart, the flow became a torrent, so strong that it pushed aside the hurts, allowing me to embrace the true love of my Father. Now I sometimes get butterflies in my stomach when I get a glimpse of his love over me. Like I'm his favorite kid! We should all feel like we're his favorite - God is that big.

I hope you are one of the lucky ones that has a caring, loving daddy in the world. If so, maybe you need to be like that mountain brook and flow some of your love his way. If not, then I hope you have discovered your spiritual Father's love, and let him minister to you as a loving Father. I think you might be one of his favorite kids!

Papa God, thank you for being a Father to the fatherless. Thank you for making us feel like we're your favorite kids. Amen

Drenched With Blessings

Life's not about waiting for the storm to pass, it's about getting out there and dancing in the rain. ~*Unknown*

Proverbs 28:20 TPT
Life's blessings drench the honest and faithful person...

Our spiritual journey with God has both mountain top experiences and dry valleys. When you're in the Mountain top place, you feel drenched with blessings every day. I remember my first few years of following the Lord felt magical like that. I saw the Lord moving on my behalf in big and little things all the time. For example, getting stuck in the snow with my baby one day. I was going over a hill in my little beetle, and the wheels start spinning on the icy road. I was blocking rush hour traffic and couldn't move an inch. Suddenly someone comes out of no where pushing me from behind until I got to the top, and then disappeared before I could say thank you!

When we find ourselves in the valleys, where it feels like God has forgotten us, it's not really what it seems. We can rejoice even then, because we know that we have grown so much in him that we no longer require "milk", and he wants us to strengthen and mature in our faith and move us to a deeper level in our walk with him. I still have many God moments when I see him pouring blessings into my life, but he is maturing me so that I also have the experiences that I can use to comfort others. He takes time to bring my hurts to the surface so I'm not dragging them into the future. He builds my character by trials as well, so that when harder things come, I won't be shaken. We know he always has our best in mind, so we need to trust in that when we find ourselves climbing out of a valley.

Lord, help me to trust you more in the valleys, and look forward to dancing in the rain on the mountain tops! Amen

Fresh Dew

In the blade of grass, in every dew drop, you witness the glory of God ~ *Sunita Sharma*

Deut. 32:2 NIV
Let my teaching fall like rain and my words descend like dew,
like showers on new grass, like abundant rain on tender plants.

I am a parent of an only child, and my daughter has always been the love of my life (next to Jesus). Every moment of her growing years were a wonder to me, and especially when she crossed that early learning threshold. She was so smart as a child! Soaking up everything and asking a million questions. Preschool became boring for her, so we enrolled her in kindergarten early at 4 1/2 years old. She went on to graduate high school with honors, and then graduated college with a double-major. I am so proud of her. What a beautiful gift from God.

Don't you wonder if Papa God brags about us that way? I think he does. I believe he loves it when we apply ourselves to learn his ways, and that he will rain down all the lessons we want to learn, like abundant rain on tender plants. We have to take those lessons a step at a time though, first drinking in the "milk" of the Word, before we will be ready for the "meat". If we try to understand it all at once, we'll be like a toddler trying to take a college course, and feeling like it's over our head. But if we take our time, reading, praying and meditating on the scriptures, we'll gain wisdom and understanding in a way that we can comprehend and build on. Our journey with God is not a crash course. It's a lifetime of learning. The world is in a hurry, but Papa God never is. I want to encourage you to slow down a bit when it comes to reading the Word, and tune the ears of your heart to hear what the Spirit is saying.

Father, I love the way there are always new things to learn in your scriptures, and in nature. Help me to keep my heart teachable. Amen

Born of Water and Spirit

(born)² ~*Cool Christian Symbol*

John 3:5 NLV
Jesus replied, "I assure you, no one can enter the
Kingdom of God without being born of water and the
Spirit. Humans can reproduce only human life, but the
Holy Spirit gives birth to spiritual life."

Witnessing the birth of a baby is an amazing experience. A new life coming into the world, born out of water. A baby comes into the world after the long wait during pregnancy, very vulnerable and helpless, depending on family to help it survive and grow. We enjoy watching them learn and become a little person, cheering them on as they go, hoping we have steered them in the right direction to have a loving, successful and healthy life beyond our care as parents. We share our faith values too, hoping they will take the most important step on their own convictions, to experience the second birth, and continue on their spiritual journey with Jesus.

In many ways, our second birth experience is much the same. There is a waiting period for us to be ready to make the choice to surrender and follow God, which happens at various times of life for different people. But when we do, it's an amazing experience. A new life, set free from all the bondages of a sinful world, and born of the Spirit. The church teaches and guides us in our journey, and gives us a family of believers for support. Can't you picture Papa God enjoying every step we take in the right direction, steering us toward greater spiritual awareness and growing our faith? Hoping we will stand firm to the end to obtain the crown of life, to hear him say "well done", and to live with him forever?

What an amazing journey Lord. Thank you for keeping me on track, and finishing the work you began in me. Amen

A Well Watered Garden

The glory of gardening: hands in the dirt, head in the sun, heart with nature. To nurture a garden is to feed not just the body, but the soul. ~ *Alfred Austin*

Isaiah 58:11 NIV
The Lord will guide you always; He will satisfy your needs in a sun-scorched land and will strengthen your frame. You will be like a well-watered garden, like a spring whose waters never fail.

Gardening has become one of my favorite things to do. It's so rewarding to work the earth in seed time, and nurture all the growing things along to harvest. The most important thing that makes a garden thrive, is abundant water. For me, gardening is also great therapy. Connecting with nature is almost a holy thing... the first job God gave man to do was to work the land and take care of it (Genesis 2:15). I spend about an hour or so a day watering and preening over my garden during growing season. When the garden is well watered, it not only is beautiful and healthy, but it gives me delicious produce and flowers that feed my body and soul, and make me happy.

I love the passage in Isaiah 58 today. What a beautiful picture of God's love for us... a well-watered garden. But don't forget to read the part before this promise. IF we do not oppress people, stop finger pointing and malicious talk, THEN our night will become like noonday, and the Lord will guide us and satisfy our needs. Somehow he always brings things around full circle, where our blessings come from blessing others. This spiritual principle is essentially the Golden Rule - to do unto others as you would have them do unto you. It sounds so easy, but our sinful nature isn't always so cooperative. We need to intentionally be kind and serve others first, to receive the outpouring of our own blessings. See if there isn't someone in your path today that you can intentionally show favor to. Part of the reward we get, is bringing joy to someone else.

Father I love how simple and yet sublime this principle is. Thank you for making things easy to understand, and apply. Help me to humble myself before others to bring your promises around full circle. Amen

Waters Week Five Reflections and Journaling Points

Write your reflections of the readings from the last week.

Love Flows Like Water: Write about your loving Father.

Drenched with Blessings: Write about your blessings.

Fresh Dew: How do you take time to grow your faith.

Born of Water and Spirit: Describe your (Born)² experience.

A Well Watered Garden: How can you be intentionally kinder?

Other Reflections

Waters Week Six

Plenty of Water

There's nothing more important than the Earth, the sky and the water. ~River Phoenix

Psalm 104:10-13 TMT
You started the springs and rivers, sent them flowing among the hills. All the wild animals now drink their fill.. Along the riverbanks the birds build nests, ravens make their voices heard. You water the mountains from your heavenly cisterns; Earth is supplied with plenty of water.

I n my lifetime, I've noticed the Earth going through cycles of drought and plenty when it comes to water. One part of our country will be in flood stage, and another part will have lakes drying up. Then after some years pass, the situation might be reversed for the same areas. Droughts in any area can be tough for mankind. We don't have the ease of migration that wildlife does when food or water gets scarce, because our infrastructure is dependent on local water sources. We might have to get creative and conservative to get through those times, but God's word tells us there will always be plenty of water - and he's given us the intelligence to be creative in getting through the cycles of nature.

We can learn a personal lesson from looking at nature's cycles, because our lives will go through times of plenty and lack as well. Sometimes we might need to think outside the box and get creative to get through tight places. It's the basic way of the world, and when we can see it as that, we can skip the drama and stress and simply adjust. I know it's not always that easy. In fact sometimes life is pretty darn hard! But the good news is, we have God on our side, and that makes all the difference. Maybe it starts with looking for the the good in every situation. "Whatever is pure, whatever is lovely, whatever is admirable, if anything is excellent or praiseworthy, think about such things." (Phil 4:8 NIV) Hard cycles in life only get harder when we are negative. Do you need to look on the bright side about something today? Remember, this too shall pass.

Papa God, thank you for being there for us through the thick and thin times of our lives. Help us to stay focused on the good things. Amen

Water and Spirit Baptism

The Holy Spirit is a seal in the lives of believers. In the ancient world, a seal was a legal signature attesting ownership and validating what was sealed.
~ *salvationprosperity.net*

Acts 1:4-5 NIV

Do not leave Jerusalem, but wait for the gift my Father promised, which you have heard me speak about. For John baptized with water, but in a few days you will be baptized with the Holy Spirit.

Baptism is a strange tradition in the Christian culture when you think about it. It's a way to show the world we are entering into our new life with Christ when we come up out of the water. It's a very spiritual experience when mixed with faith. I've actually been baptized in water twice. The first time, when I was first "born again", was in a city park lake. The second time was with my husband, right after our marriage in a deep river. The second time was a really special moment, because it felt like we were coming up out of the water as "one" with God.

Jesus mentioned another baptism with the Holy Spirit, and asked the disciples to wait for it before starting their ministry. The Holy Spirit was going to give them the power to do ministry on a whole new level. When I learned about this, I wanted it, even though I didn't quite understand how it worked. My experience was a prayer among friends who laid hands on me, asking the Lord to anoint me with this gift, and me leaning in to receive it. I can't say that I had some amazing spiritual thing happen that day, but the days that followed gave me the evidence of walking out my faith with more power and confidence. A "knowing" that I didn't have before. It's difficult to define, but I sensed the Lord's presence in my life in a new way. I also began to have a stronger sense of discernment that I consider a gift as well. I believe it's a very personal and individual experience, so it may be different for everyone. I only know that my life has never been the same since. You can read all about it in the book of acts. Are you ready to take the next step?

Holy Spirit, what a blessing to know you, to have your comfort, your counsel, and your gifts. Thank you.

Like Spring Rain

May the flowers remind us why the rain was so necessary.
~Ian Oku

Hosea 6:3 NLT
So keep on trying to know the Lord. His coming to us is as sure as the rising of the sun. He will come to us like the rain, like the spring rain giving water to the earth.

I truly love the Spring when every growing thing is waking up from winter and coming alive again. My bulbs are blooming, the fruit trees are flowering and leafing out, and the meadow grass is a foot tall, and waving in the breeze. I begin a daily routine of going out to the garden to watch it grow and pamper it. I do a lot of weeding, pruning and trimming. I plant new things and clean out the beds to allow nothing to hinder my herbs and veggies. I am already looking forward to the bountiful harvest coming.

This passage in Hosea reminds us that the Lord is coming, just a sure as the rising of the sun, and the spring season that comes again every year. He's also like the rain that causes everything to grow and flourish in that season. I love that comparison, because Spring is always our hope to get through the cold winter, and the Lord's coming is our hope to get us through this entire journey called life, and bring us to what lies beyond. Our Father is like the tender gardener, weeding and pruning us to prepare us for the time of harvest, when our Jesus comes to gather us to himself. Then we'll see what has been prepared for us; a paradise we can't even imagine. Today, let yourself be reminded of the good things Papa God has in store for us, and remember we are only foreigners living in this land. Jesus will bring us home one day, when he comes to us like the Spring rain.

Lord Jesus, thank you for the reassurance that gives us the hope that lives in our hearts. We look for your return to bring us home. Amen

Garden Beside a River

In all this world there is nothing as beautiful as a happy child. ~ *L. Frank Baum*

How beautiful are your children... like gardens beside a river...
like aloes planted by the Lord... like cedars beside the waters...

You can't help but notice how the area around rivers have flourishing green growth, big healthy trees, and colorful wild flowers. It looks like Gods happy little garden. I love to take walks in the Spring and Summer and gather wild flowers along our road to dress up my front porch. I say, "Thank you Lord for that pretty bouquet"!

It's beautiful to think that Papa God sees us like a "garden beside a river", and it's really how we need to see ourselves too. The Bible says over and over again, that his children have special favor and that he will cause them to flourish. I think he loves to see his children loving life like a little child. In fact statistics show that believers are generally happier people. An article on Time[dot]com says: "Study after study has found that religious people tend to be less depressed and less anxious than nonbelievers..." Another article from Daily Philosophy says, "Religion has a profound effect on happiness. Multiple studies have shown that religious believers are generally happier people..." If you have not been feeling like the "happy little child" described here, maybe you need to shake off any heaviness, and embrace the Lord's favor again. Picture yourself like a big cedar tree beside the waters soaking up God's goodness.

Thank you Father for blessing your people with divine favor. Help us become like little children, looking with wonder at your creation. (Matt 18) Amen

Memories of the Sea

The scent of the water, and the sound of the sea, makes me ever so happy, just to be me. ~coastalbeachstyle.com

Some of my best teen and early adult memories are at the beach. Growing up in southern Cal, weekends at the beach was the norm. To this day the sound and smell of the ocean takes me back to those days.

One of my favorite times was a day at the beach with my younger sister when we were in our late teens. She and I were close in those days, and I didn't know I had so little time left with her. She was the first to find Jesus, and used to nag me to come to church with her regularly. At first I shrugged it off and said it wasn't my thing, but as time went on, and I found myself lost in the storms of life, I started to change my mind. I wished she would ask me to go with her again, but wouldn't you know it, she stopped asking. I finally had to break down and ask if I could go with her, because I knew I was ready to meet Jesus too. The next years we had together were even more special, sharing our faith, family, and lives until job moves separated us by many miles. Before we knew it, 10 years had gone by with hardly a visit, and then a serious health issue suddenly took her life. Those days at the beach now mean even more to me.

Life and death are a reality in this life, and it's never easy to lose someone you love. But, because she knew the Lord, the memories of crashing waves don't make me sad; they sound more like the celebration of her life. The sea is shouting with praise about her going home! Isn't it amazing how God can make heaven and Earth sing to our hearts in so many different ways? Today, listen carefully to hear a new song in your heart. It might change a sad memory into a song of praise.

Thank you Papa God, for holding our loved ones in your gaze, and giving us sweet memories to hold on to while we wait to meet them again. Amen

Waters Week Six Reflections and Journaling Points

Write your reflections of the readings from the last week.

<u>Plenty of Water:</u> *How the Lord provides for you..*

<u>Water and Spirit Baptism:</u> *Notes about your baptisms.*

<u>Like Spring Rain:</u> *How is the Father pruning you?*

<u>Garden Beside a River:</u> *Shake off heaviness, become a child.*

<u>Memories of the Sea:</u> *Turning sad memories into praises.*

<u>Other Reflections</u>

Skies
HOW BIG IS OUR GOD

Introduction

⟡

The Sky is a reminder that many things are possible even though they seem beyond our reach. ~ *Brandon Royal*

Psalm 19:1 NIV
"The Heavens declare the glory of God."

I love spending time in nature and the great outdoors. It's wonderful to have a bright sunny day when you plan an outing, but I also appreciate the cloudy and rainy days for road trips as well. It gives a whole new perspective to see nature in the elements. But clear skies are really the best for viewing the stars at night.

Our God is truly an artist. All of planet Earth has its beauty to behold, but the skies are the cherry on top. The grandness of the skies above with all the color and forms in the clouds from sunrise to sunset is sometimes jaw dropping beautiful. And looking out into the universe on a clear night is humbling. It's the place where God lives. I can't help feeling very small and insignificant when I see the vastness of what the night sky reveals.

Just as in all of nature, the skies have lessons to teach us too. God uses all of it to tutor us along in our walk though life and our spiritual journey as well. We see peaceful sunsets, and loud, scary thunderstorms. We gaze at the stars, and learn of signs in the heavens. What does it all mean to God's children? I hope to shed some light on these things, with the help of the Holy Spirit, to encourage and inspire you in your daily walk. I hope these pages help you slow down a bit and take another look at how the skies reflect the creator. He has so much to say to us through His creation!

Lord bless you in your journey. ~Linda!

Skies
Week One

Starry Nights

I like the night. Without the dark, we'd never see the stars. ~*Stephenie Meyer*

Psalm 16: 7 & 9 TVT
I will bless the Eternal, whose wise teaching orchestrates
my days and centers my mind at night... This is a good life
- my heart is glad, my soul is full of joy, and my body is at
rest. Who could want for more?

Sometimes when I can't sleep, I step outside on our deck to check out the stars. If it's summer time, I'll lay back on the chair and just gaze at the amazing universe for a while, talking to my Father. There is a magical effect the starry night can have on your soul - it makes me feel so small, and I realize just how big our God is. We forget so easily in the busy bustle of our days, but seeing how big the universe is helps me to realize how small my problems really are in the grand scheme of things

After my 'middle of the night' reflections, I can usually get some good rest and feel refreshed in the morning. I can't say enough about how important it is to get these quiet times of reflection, to share our thoughts with the creator of the universe and listen intently for His response. The next time you can't sleep, and it's a clear night, go take a peek at the starry night, and let your heart be moved to draw closer to God.

Oh Lord my God... how majestic are your works! Thank you for centering my mind at night and giving my body the rest it needs. Amen

Sunset Beauty

Sunsets are proof that no matter what happens, every day can end beautifully. *~Kristen Butler*

Psalm 115: 16 TVT
The heavens above belong to the Eternal, and yet Earth in
all of its beauty has been given to humanity by Him.

Everyone enjoys a beautiful sunset, and I think the best sunsets are in the mountains. Nothing makes me stop and wonder at pure beauty than a colorful sunset. Even though I try to share them with others, pictures can rarely capture the moments of these events. What a gift has been given to us! "The Earth in all of its beauty." Sunsets make me stop and say, Thank You!

Have you ever stopped to contemplate how the God of the Universe made all of this for His pleasure, and then gave it all to humanity? He gave it to us, and gave us dominion over it. What a bold move! He must really love us. Sadly, not all our decisions have been good for planet Earth, and not all our decisions have been to follow the creator who gave it all to us. But it was always his intention that we would discover him, that we would seek the truth about him. But it has to be our intention to find him - and when we do seek to know him with our whole hearts, he will be found. He will reveal himself to us. He will give us His Holy Spirit to connect us forever to him. Let's make sure the little part of the planet given to each of us represents him well.

Father God, I am overwhelmed by the grace you give us in the beauty of planet Earth. Help me to steward it well. Amen

Heavens Praise Him

All nature seems to bespeak the works of God.
~*Boyd K. Packer*

Psalm 148 NLT
Praise the Lord from the heavens! Praise him
from the skies!... Praise him, sun and moon!
Praise him, all you twinkling stars!..

I truly love gathering together with believers for praise and worship. Nothing is sweeter than a gathering of people united in heart and purpose, and worshiping in spirit and truth. When the Spirit of the Lord is present and our hearts are so full they spill over into a love for our God that can't be expressed in words... it's, well, beyond words for me to explain! But we are not alone... all of creation gives praise to our God in its own way. Even the sun, the moon and the stars!

Now I know that the world at large may think of me as a fanatic, and maybe I am. It's ok that some don't understand. My eyes have been opened. I decided long ago to be 'all in', and that was really the beginning of my life's journey. You see, "faith is not a conclusion you reach, it's a journey you live." (Quote from AW Tozer) Deciding to follow God and surrender my life to him is only the start of a great adventure. Steven Curtis Chapman wrote one of my favorite songs called the 'Great Adventure', and it goes like this: "Saddle up your horses - we've got a trail to blaze! Through the wild blue yonder of God's amazing grace. Let's follow our leader into the glorious unknown... this is a life like no other, whoa whoa, this is the Great Adventure! So come on get ready, for the ride of your life... gonna leave long faced religion in a cloud of dust behind, and discover all the new horizons waiting to be explored... this is what we were created for..!" Yes! That's the life I'm talking about!! Are you ready to ride?

Papa God, I love living for you. It's not a perfect life, but there is no where I'd rather be. Teach me, guide me, show me more of you. Amen

Peaceful Skies

Peace is seeing the sunrise or a sunset,
and knowing who to thank.
An Amish Proverb

John 20:21-22 TVT
I give you the gift of peace. In the same way the Father sent me, I am now sending you. Now he drew close enough to each of them that they could feel his breath. He breathed on them and said, welcome the Holy Spirit of the living God.

Finding calm and peace in a beautiful sunset is something everyone can do. It's a matter of stopping everything to capture this moment of beauty that is passing by in the sky. Most days we are much too busy to do that, although nature offers it up regardless of who takes the time to notice. I love them so much, I purposefully seek them out. I have even joined online groups that post beautiful sunsets from around the world, to enjoy them from the comfort of my computer screen.

The Spirit of God is a lot like a beautiful sunset... it's available for anyone to receive, but we must seek him out and stop everything to set our attention and desires toward the Spirit's call on our lives. For it is a calling, and not something we could just grab on our own. The Holy Spirit of the Living God is a gift given by Jesus, and received by those who seek him out. How can I begin to describe this gift? The scripture above is the closest explanation I can give. We welcome the Holy Spirit flowing into our hearts, and therein enters Peace - the 'knowing' that it is well with our soul. I have aligned with my Creator. It's probably the biggest life changing event anyone can have. It changes everything, because we are never the same. Have you asked for - and received the precious Holy Spirit?

Holy Spirit of the Living God - fall afresh on me. Amen

New Day Dawning

Today is not just another day. It's a new opportunity,
another chance, a new beginning. Embrace it..
~kushandwizdom blog

2 Cor 5:18 TPT
God has made all things new, and reconciled us to himself, and given us the ministry of reconciling others to God.

When ever I'm on a road trip that takes several days to get to my destination, I like to rise before the dawn and get out on the road with a fresh, hot cup of coffee so I can see the sun rise as I drive. It's like witnessing the birth of 'today'. When I'm on the road, far from home and work and all the stress that goes with it, I can really sense the freshness of a new day dawning with all its possibilities.

For a time I was involved in a recovery ministry that worked with women coming out of addictions. That lifestyle can leave a life in ruins, but I always tried to encourage the ladies to remember that today was a new day, and they could leave yesterday behind and start over. With God's help, every new day gives us another chance to get it right and make good decisions. We may have to live with the consequences of our bad decisions, but the decisions we make today will make our tomorrows better. And when you add God to that equation, it's a win-win. In fact, you can't lose!

Not only has the Lord made everything new in my life and given me the ability to start over with his love and grace backing me up, but he gives me the ministry of helping others find their way to him and recovery as well. What a blessing to be able to take the comfort that I received and learned from surrendering my life to Jesus, and share it with others. What have you been through that could comfort others in their struggles?

Thank you Lord for new beginnings, and for using me to speak into the lives of others. Amen

Skies Week One Reflections and Journaling Points

Write your reflections of the readings from the last week.

Starry Nights: Quiet moments that move you closer to God.

Sunset Beauty: Looking for God in the beauty of the skies.

The Heavens Praise: Stepping into the 'Great Adventure'.

Peaceful Skies: Setting our attention on the Spirit of God.

New Day Dawning: How your new beginning comforts others.

Other Reflections

Skies
Week Two

The Stars Speak

The Milky Way Galaxy is an immense and very interesting place. Not only does it measure some 120,000-180,000 light-years in diameter, it is home to planet Earth, the birthplace of humanity. ~*UniverseToday.com*

The celestial realms announce God's glory; the skies testify of His hands' great work. Each day pours out more of their sayings; each night, more to hear and more to learn. Inaudible words are their manner of speech, their means to convey.

When I was younger I used to love to go camping in the desert - in the cooler months - just because it was the best place to see the stars at night. We would drive down a dirt road into the deep desert, as far away from city lights as possible. On a moonless night the stars are amazing. It was only a matter of time before you could see a shooting star, or two or three.

The Word says that God stretched out the stars in the heavens, and placed the sun in its place; everything in perfect position to sustain life on planet Earth. Science and modern technology reveal more and more every day about an intelligent design in the universe. We know so much about the ways of the universe, that it takes more faith to believe in Darwin's theory at this point, but sadly most people would rather believe a lie than have to admit there is really a Creator. Romans 1:20 says "For since the creation of the world God's invisible qualities - his eternal power and divine nature - have been clearly seen, being understood from what has been made..." I didn't grow up in a godly home, and too many go through life without knowing about our Creator. When public schools are teaching our kids evolution, let's make sure our kids know the truth, every opportunity we get.

Father, God of Creation, thank you for this amazing planet you made just for us. I ask you for wisdom and knowledge to present the truth about creation when ever the opportunity arises. Amen

Flowing Winds

I can't change the direction of the wind, but I can adjust
my sails to always reach my destination. *~Jimmy Dean*

Galations 1:3 TPT
I pray over you a release of the blessings of God's undeserved kindness and total well-being that flows from our Father-God and from the Lord Jesus.

If you're a parent, you know the feeling of pure love waving over your being when you have a little one asleep on your chest, and you realize what a gift you've been given. It's so real, it's almost tangible, like a wind blowing over your soul. If you're not a parent, perhaps you've experienced that moment you know you have fallen in love, and are loved back. This is the closest thing I can think of to explain how it feels when the presence of the Holy Spirit moves. Like the breath of God blowing blessings right into your life. Feeling like you are standing in the presence of a Holy God is an awesome, scary, wonderful and blessed thing. Sometimes it's overwhelming, and we break down emotionally or even become physically weak. Others might laugh or cry - at the same time! But it always leaves you hungry for more.

There have been times in my life that I've known without a doubt that the Lord's favor was upon me, or that I just had a 'divine appointment' with chance meetings. The more you know the Father, the Son and the sweet Holy Spirit, the more you'll recognize his moves and touches. Some people want to explain away things I give God credit for, but I know my Father's voice, my Father's love. I pray this will be a season you will sense the Lord's blessings and undeserved kindness flowing into your life. I pray you will have that total well-being that springs from knowing your Papa God. The more we seek to know him, the more he reveals to us. May your heart always be hungry for more.

"There's nothing worth more, that will ever come close, nothing can compare, You're our living hope. your presence, Lord." (Song by Jesus Culture)

Promises

As long as the Earth endures, seedtime and harvest,
cold and heat, summer and winter, day and night
will never cease. ~*Genesis 8:22 NIV*

Galations 3:14 TPT
...And now God gives us the promise of the wonderful Holy Spirit who lives within us when we believe in him.

The beauty and promise of the rainbow is a universal sign to everyone on planet Earth. It's always a special moment when you glimpse one, and they can disappear so quickly, you have to keep your eyes glued to it, to see it just a few seconds longer. It's like a little bit of heaven come to Earth. A sign from God that he will never again flood the whole Earth. Make sure your children know the real biblical meaning of the rainbow.

There are so many wonderful promises in the Bible. Some of them are related to creation and the laws of nature that apply to everyone - like seedtime and harvest, day and night, the seasons. Other promises have to do with spiritual things - a loving Father, gifts of faith, and eternal life. They're like hidden treasures waiting for us to find and claim for our own. But by far the greatest promise we can welcome into our hearts, is the wonderful Holy Spirit. This is the first spiritual promise to manifest when we step out in faith and accept Jesus as our Savior. The promise that the the Spirit of the Living God will live within us, so that we know we are his. This is the common element all believer's share that is unexplainable to the world culture. It's just one of those things that will never be understood until it's experienced.

Thank you Father for all your promises, but especially your precious Holy Spirit within me. Use me Lord to help others to seek and find you. Amen

A Flood of Light

I cannot cause light; the most I can do is try to put myself in the path of its beam. ~ *Annie Dillard*

Eph 1:18 TPT
I pray that the light of God will illuminate the eyes
of your imagination, flooding you with light, until
you experience the full revelation of the hope of his calling
- that is, the wealth of God's glorious inheritances..

During the rainy season where I live, the cloudy days can last weeks. After a few days, I start to long for the warmth of the sun. After a week, I'm beginning to feel ansy. When the cloudy days last weeks, I'm looking for a way out. I remember one time in my twenties, I got so depressed after a month of cloudy weather, that I got in my car and drove for miles to the east to get out from under the cloud. When I finally found the sunlight, I pulled over and stood with my face in the sun. It lasted for three minutes, and the clouds were back. So I drove further, and got out in the sun again. Ten minutes later the clouds were back! I gave up and drove back home. Wouldn't you know it, as I was getting close to home, I saw the clouds had parted and the sun was shining through in big beams of light. It was a sunny day at home, and I missed it.

I wonder if that is what sometimes happens when we try to make things happen instead of waiting on God. I went chasing after that thing I was obsessed about, and found that God's glory was behind me, and I was missing my moment. God is so patient with us, waiting our lifetime for us to seek him so he can send that illuminating light across our path, so we will see and understand the hope that is in Christ, and reach out and grab hold of it. Afterwards, we can bask in the light of his presence, until we get the full revelation of his calling. Let's be careful we aren't rushing ahead and running past what God has for us.

Papa God, I long to bask in your light. To feel the warmth of your presence, and have the eyes of my imagination be flooded with the light of your truths and your plans. Help me to not run ahead and miss anything you have for me. Amen

Clear Blue Sky

If the sight of the blue skies fills you with joy, if a blade of
grass springing up in the fields, has the power to move
you, if the simple things of nature have a message that
you understand, rejoice, for your soul is alive.
~ *Eleonora Duse*

Proverbs 3:5 TPT
Trust in the Lord completely, and do not rely on your own
opinions. With all your heart rely on him to guide you,
and he will lead you in every decision you make.
Become intimate with him in whatever you do,
and he will lead you wherever you go.

The forest is so beautiful when there is a clear blue sky. The trees and mountains seem to touch the sky and make a picture post card of the day. It's a great way to start your day, especially when your heart is heavy with big decisions to make. A sunny day somehow makes me feel lighter.

Have you ever put out a 'fleece' to the Lord about a big decision? One day I got a big idea that I felt came from the Lord. I felt strongly that God would either open or closed doors in my situation. I needed to make a decision about a big investment in a new retirement career. I had big dreams on the line here. If my offer was accepted, I knew God was in it, otherwise I would walk away. The other party tried to get me to budge off my offer, but I would not, and the deal ended up falling through. I could have made some concessions to make it happen, but I didn't, because I trusted the Lord completely about the fleece. Worse than my dreams not coming true, was making a life changing decision without knowing my Father's blessing was on it.

Now I'm not suggesting that a fleece is a formula for testing the Spirit's wishes. It doesn't work like that. The point is, if you're going to trust him to lead you, you cannot waver. He hates it when we waver and sit on the fence about our faith. Is there something you need to take a faith stand on today? If we trust in him, then we can't be disappointed if it doesn't go the way we hoped. We can trust that he has a different plan for us.

Father, thank you for leading me wherever I go. I can rely on you with all my heart to lead me into the best path for my life. Amen

Skies Week Two Reflections and Journaling Points

Write your reflections of the readings from the last week.

The Stars Speak:. *Sharing the truth of creation.*

Flowing Winds: *The presence of the Lord brings favor.*

Promises: *The promise of the Holy Spirit living in us.*

A Flood of Light: *Waiting on God and basking in His light.*

Clear Blue Sky: *Prayers and fleeces. Stepping out in faith.*

Other Reflections

Skies
Week Three

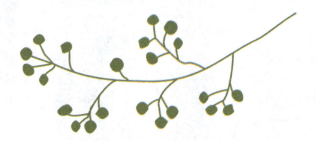

Morning Light

Give every day the chance to become the most beautiful day of your life. ~*Mark Twain*

Proverbs 4:18 TPT
But the lovers of God walk on the highway of light,
and their way shines brighter until they
bring forth the perfect day.

Watching the morning light coming into the forest from my windows is one of my favorite daily events. I'm an early bird, so I usually get up just as the sky is getting lighter. My internal clock somehow senses the light in the room, and I'm awake. I will get the coffee brewing and feed the cat, then settle in my comfy corner to wait for the sun to break over the hill and into my living room. This is the setting for our morning devotions, and it's a great way to start the day.

How the rest of the day goes, is another story. Stuff happens to get in the way of our perfect day, doesn't it? But I'm learning that the perfect day still belongs to me, if I will only stay on the "highway of light". I don't have to let the stress and disappointments pressing in, dictate my mood. I know that sounds too simplistic, and I don't mean to suggest we can all live in a state of happiness all the time. But God's word always speaks about how we have the power to overcome the world, and there's a nagging notion in my head and heart that says all I have to do is figure it out. Just tap into the power of God almighty living on the inside of me, and boom! I've got it. The passage above says that I will bring forth the perfect day. Could it be about how I shine into other's lives too? As I walk through my day, my light can shine into those around me, bringing them closer to their own perfect day. It's a beautiful thing to enlighten someone else's path. Even if your day does not flow perfectly, I encourage you to look for ways to shine some light onto someone's path today. You'll find that will make yours a little brighter too. Boom!

Father, help me to give this day the chance to become a beautiful day for someone you put across my path, and thank you for causing that shared light to make my day a little brighter too. Amen.

Beams of Light

Even a small beam of light is an immense hope. No matter how intense the darkness is... *~Maira*

188

Proverbs 6:23 TPT
For truth is a bright beam of light shining into every area
of your life, instructing and correcting you to discover the
ways to godly living.

The dictionary describes "Conscience" as an inner feeling or voice viewed as acting as a guide to the rightness or wrongness of one's behavior. Someone who has their conscience seared means they no longer have that inner voice telling them wrong from right any more. I believe that was the way God found me back in the day. My life was a bit of a mess back then, to put it mildly. But a funny thing happened when I started searching for the truth about God. Looking back, I believe he was shining those beams of light, mentioned in Proverbs 6, into my spirit to wake up my conscience to the truth. It was a bit annoying, actually, because once my conscience softened up a bit, I just couldn't enjoy the things I used to. The more I was seeking God, the more doing things against my conscience bothered me. It finally got to the point that I had to walk away from those things that didn't sit right with my conscience. I came to realize there was real freedom in doing the right thing. Eventually I came to treasure my clear conscience.

There are some people in the world that seem so far away from God, we might think they are beyond hope. But even a small beam of light can change their hard heart. For me, my little sister was that light, although there were many others that planted seeds of faith along the way. How precious it is to speak life and light into a darkened heart. Is there someone in your circle of influence that needs a little beam of light?

Dear Lord, thank you for the times you sent your light shining into my heart. Lord, keep sending those beams into the dark places, instructing and correcting and helping me discover the way to live for you. And help me to shine that light and love back into the hearts of others. Amen

A Dry Season

...I'll tell you one more thing about dry seasons: they don't last forever. This season will change. Just keep the faith, keep trusting him, keep going to church, keep praising and worshiping God even when it's hard and confusing. The rain is coming. *iBelieve.com*

Proverbs 10:5 TPT
Know the importance of the season you're in, and a wise son you will be. But what a waste when an incompetent son sleeps through his day of opportunity!

In nature, the dry spells can be devastating. The clouds go by without leaving a drop of water, and the growing things begin to wither. Gardens struggle, and it takes extra TLC to keep things alive. Life requires adjustments during a dry season to get through it, but the good news is that the season does pass eventually.

The last couple years living in a pandemic have been like a very dry season for the entire planet. The lock down mandates at the beginning isolated us. Businesses and churches closed, friends & family segregated, and lives withered and died in the wake of a sickness that we were totally unprepared for. As time went by, we made adjustments and found out just how resilient we could be in a challenging season. How we come out on the other side, depends on how we adjust to the season we are in.

Hard seasons can bring a change of direction, a new perspective, and require new ways to do things. I personally got a wake up call during what I thought was the worst possible time for making major decisions. But because of circumstances brought about by covid, it turned out to be the best time to make the move. I saw the opportunity to take advantage of the good that could come out of it. Even in a dry and hurting place, the Spirit of God can speak blessings to us, when we are looking for him. Keep your eyes and heart focused on what the Lord is doing in every season, and never be afraid to follow where he leads.

Thank you Father for always working things out for our good, and showing us the importance of the seasons we are in. Amen

Spot Light

Stay true in the dark and humble in the spotlight.
~*Quoteistan.com*

Proverbs 13:9 TPT
The virtues of God's lovers shine brightly in the darkness.

Beams of sunlight through the clouds have a magical quality about them. It's like God himself is pointing his finger through the clouds to highlight the beauty of his creation. But let's not forget that as beautiful as planet Earth is, we (you & me) are actually what he considers his masterpiece. When we are living a righteous life, he says our virtues shine out just like a beam of sunlight.

Our light was always meant to reflect back on the Creator and brighten up the dark places of the world. Our virtues of love, faith and compassion bring to light the truth about the Creator.

I've heard it said that we should always share our faith, using words, only when necessary. The world is watching us, and they love to poke fun and often disrespect the Lord we love. It's a self-protection reaction from a carnal mindset, and I remember it well. I resisted anything to do with God for some time when I was young. It was just going to be too much to admit I was wrong, and what a sinner I really was.

There were many people that shined their lights into my life back then. A little beam of light here and there, started adding up to an undeniable reality of a need I didn't even know I had. Until finally one day I said yes to Jesus. Well, everything changed, and I've never been the same.

Is there darkness around you that needs a bit of light? It doesn't take a lot of effort when the Lord of Light is shining through you.

Father God, let your light burst forth from me like a beacon to those who need you today, whether they know it or not. Amen

Before the Sun Sets

For every minute you are angry, you lose sixty seconds of happiness. ~ *Ralph Waldo Emerson*

Ephesians 4:26 TVT
Don't let the sun set with anger in your heart or give the devil room to work.

Sunsets at the end of any day are beautiful, but sometimes we might be too preoccupied to take time to see them. Today's society moves at a fast pace, and our busyness distracts us from enjoying these moments of beauty. The Lord warns us about how some distractions can even give the devil a foothold in our lives. Anger. Not all anger is bad, as there is a "righteous" anger we feel when injustices happen. But this is not the subject of Ephesians 4:26. Anger in our hearts that we hold on to will open the door for evil to enter in.

So how do we let it go? Sometimes these emotions seem to have a grip on us, don't they? Well, the answer is very simple. Graciously forgive. Be kind and compassionate. Just as God has forgiven us. Ouch. We sometimes feel justified in our attitudes. I admit that I've struggled with this issue, but over time I've learned that the sooner I let it go, the sooner I can get back to a happy life. Remember, the enemy of our souls comes to steal, kill and destroy our joy in life. Knowing this is what makes it easier to dismiss the bad attitudes, and the Holy Spirit will help by giving us the power to overcome.

We can speak out Romans 15:13 to reclaim our joy. "God, fill me with all joy and peace as I trust in you, by the power of the Holy Spirit." Our mouth speaks, our ears hear, and the word of God cannot go out without accomplishing what it was sent to do. Also, a new attitude makes it easier to forgive. Try it next time you need an attitude adjustment.

Holy Spirit, thank you for the power to overcome the spirit of anger. Help me to forgive all wrongs before I lay my head down, and protect me from the evil one. I repent of allowing that spirit to enter in, and I ask you to replace it with your joy and peace. Amen

Skies Week Three Reflections and Journaling Points

Write your reflections of the readings from the last week.

<u>*Morning Light:*</u>. *Bringing forth a perfect day with God's light.*

<u>*Beams of Light:*</u> *There is freedom in doing what is right.*

<u>*Dry Seasons:*</u> *A change of direction?*

<u>*Spot Lights:*</u> *Shining some light into someone's life.*

<u>*Before the Sun Sets:*</u> *Letting go of bad attitudes..*

<u>*Other Reflections*</u>

Skies
Week Four

Search Lights

There are two ways of spreading the light: to be the candle or the mirror that reflects it. *~Edith Wharton*

Proverbs 20:27 TPT
The spirit God breathed into man is like a living lamp, a
shining light searching into the innermost
chamber of our being.

When I lived in Virginia many years ago, I visited a light house on the east coast of North Carolina. The light house fixtures have a unique character about them. They use big curved mirrors to reflect the light out to sea. They are particularly impressive at night, streaming their beacons across the sky to guide ships to a safe dock. Wouldn't it be nice if someone would shine a light on our path to guide us in the dark places of life? Proverbs chapter 20 has the answer. The light that God breathes into us is the Holy Spirit. Here he is called a 'living lamp' shining into the innermost part of us.

In some ways, it's a little intimidating to think about the light of God exposing everything in the depths of our hearts and souls. There are some things in there I'd rather keep hidden, if I'm honest. But it seems that this journey with my Lord is a process of diving deep into those hidden places to bring them to light and be dealt with. It's the way we heal past hurts and grow in freedom and maturity. Then when we are mature, we can reflect the light we have out to the world to lead others along their paths. This is a distinct pattern with the Holy Spirit, he cleans us up, and fills us up, so we can let it flow through us to others.

Thank you Father, for shining your light into tour hearts, helping us to be freer and purer every day. Help us to shed your light into the world to light the path for others to your freedom and healing. Amen

Lightning

Humans have deified lightning for millennia *~Wikipedia*

Matthew 28:3 NIV
...for an angel of the Lord came down from heaven and
going to the tomb, rolled back the stone and sat on it.
His appearance was like lightning, and
his clothes were white as snow.

When I lived in Arizona, we would get big thunder storms during the monsoon season. It was often an occasion to get out on the porch and watch the light show in the sky. Such power and glory in the passing clouds! The torrential rain fall was so heavy we had to dig a stream bed through our property. It was amazing how much water could come down in the space of a few minutes.

It's interesting how many of the spiritual personas mentioned in the bible are described as being bright like lightning or white as snow. Just think of the power in a bolt of lightning, and how it's compared to God and angels. It's the only thing powerful enough and bright enough in our world to even come close to describing the brilliance of our God.

Have you ever seen pictures of the Shroud of Turin? It's like a photograph of Jesus on a piece of cloth. I read it's speculated it must have been a phenomenon like a big flash of light happening, when he came back to life in the tomb that made the image. No one can explain it. According to Luke, on the day Lord Jesus returns, we will see flashes of lightning in the sky from one end to the other. Luke says not to be distracted when people say he's come, because this flash of light is the clue that the whole world will see when he returns. The next time you see lightning, think about how glorious it will be on the day of the Lord. Some will wonder what it means, and others of us will know.

Thank you Father for the revelation knowledge you gave us about the momentous day in Earths history that will not take us by surprise. Prepare our hearts to be ready. Amen

Naming Stars

Stars are giant, luminous spheres of plasma. There are billions of them, including our own sun, in the Milky Way galaxy. And there are billions of galaxies in the universe.
~*space.com*

Psalm 147:4 NIV
He determines the number of the stars and calls them each by name.

I've heard there is a company that allows you to name a star, visible from Earth, after someone you love. I admit it's a romantic idea, but it's a bit audacious since God has already named all the stars. Imagine just how long that job took! It boggles the mind to consider. It took me months to figure out a name for my daughter when I was expecting.

Did you know that we will all get a new name when we get to heaven? Revelation 2:17 says, "..To the one who is victorious, I will give some of the hidden manna. I will also give that person a white stone with a new name written on it, known only to the one who receives it."

Names in the Bible always have meaning. Abraham's wife Sarah's name means "noblewoman". King Davids' name means "Beloved", and his son Solomon's name means "Peace". Jesus has seventy two different names with meanings.

It sounds like our new name will be sort of a secret name the Lord gives us, and will have a meaning that only we will know. It reminds me of how Native Americans get interesting and descriptive names based on something meaningful to them personally; like "Running Horse" or 'Stands with a fist". I wonder how the Lord will name me based on my life, personality, and spiritual attributes? I expect it will be something lovely and extremely special. It's wonderful to think about how special I am to my Father. I hope you have that feeling about Papa God as well. He named the stars, and he has a special name for you too.

I am amazed Father, at the way you name everything in a personal, individual way. Thank you for your affection toward me and every created thing. Amen

203

Light Breaking Through

❧

Sometimes hope means merely searching for the light
shining through the darkness. *~Sarah Arthur*

Isaiah 60:1-2 TVT
Arise, shine, for your light has broken through!
The Eternal's bright glory will shine on you,
a light for all to see.

Have you ever been in that place where you're looking for light shining at the end of a long dark tunnel? Life is like that sometimes. Hard times can drag on, and we long for better days that must be right around the corner, right? Well here's a new perspective: what if God is that light? He is shining over his children so brightly, that we can reflect it and be a light for others. Yes, we can be the light for others peering around the corner for relief. And the amazing thing is, that we find our own way out of the dark when we give away our light. It's the way of the Kingdom, and I love it.

I think we have an unusual gifting in us when we're around others in need. It's like magic; we forget about our problems for a moment, and an internal light comes on to shine a little love; God's love shining through us. This is the way our Father designed us to be. So if we find ourselves too caught up in our own problems to care about others, we have forgetting who we are in Christ.

We are the light of the world! It doesn't say we will be lights only when we are happy. God's light shines on us all the time. So look around. Let's forget about ourselves for a moment, and experience the magic when we become the light we were made to be. You will find it lightens the heaviness in your life too.

Jesus, you are the light that broke through for the world to see. Thank you for placing your light in us to continue to shine into a hurting world. Thank you for healing us as we reach out to others. Help us to remember who we are. Amen

A Sign in the Sky

"Sign" is a general word for whatever gives evidence of an event: past, present, or future. Dark clouds are a sign of rain or snow. ~*Dictionary.com*

Matthew 24:29-30 TVT
After the distress of those days, the sun will be darkened,
and the moon will not give its light; the
stars will fall from the sky, and the heavenly
bodies will be shaken. Then will appear the
sign of the Son of Man in heaven.

There are so many questions about end times and the sign of Jesus' coming. I've read books, watched videos, and listened to many sermons on the subject, and although there are many different possible scenarios presented, they all agree on one thing: it's coming soon. That thought used to make me a little crazy. We can get so caught up in the anticipation, that we become anxious. We are definitely living in distressed times, right? Could this be the beginning of the end? It seems like the enemy of our souls is on a roll with the fear mongering theme lately. If he can't scare us with a pandemic, maybe stressing us about the end times will get us in fear mode.

Well, we know that God our Father did not give us a spirit of fear. So I've decided to put all that aside, because I've read the book, and I know how it turns out. Also, Matthew chapter 24 gives a clear vision of what to expect, so unless I see these signs in the sky all at the same time, I won't be anticipating the sign of the Son of Man coming in the clouds. There is a lot that will happen leading up to this moment, and I can know that the time is near, but I don't have to worry or fret. We as believers have the inside scoop and our Father in his wisdom has given us a glimpse of what the plan is, so we are not taken by surprise. It feels kind of good to be "in the know" on this one, don't you agree?

Thank you Father for sharing your plan for mankind, and your children in particular. I feel loved, secure, and privileged to hold your words in my heart. Amen

Skies Week Four Reflections and Journaling Points

Write your reflections of the readings from the last week.

<u>Search Lights:</u>. *Bringing hidden places in our heart to light.*

<u>Lightning:</u> *Revelations about the day of the Lord.*

<u>Naming Stars:</u> *God has a special name for us.*

<u>Light Breaking Through:</u> *How God lightens your heaviness.*

<u>A Sign in the Sky:</u> *God tells us what to expect.*

<u>Other Reflections</u>

Skies
Week Five

Interpreting the Sky

❧

Red sky at night, sailor's delight. Red sky at morning, sailor's warning. ~ *E.E. Borton*

Matthew 16:2-4 (paraphrased) TVT
You read the red sky in the evening and morning as a sign
for weather, so you are skilled at interpreting the sky, but
you cannot interpret the signs of the times? The only sign
you will get is the sign of Jonah.

There is diverse beauty in the skies, and it is a marvel to me. Nowadays we have smart phones to tell us what the weather is going to be, but I remember the simple days when you would look outside at the sky to figure out if it was a good weather day. I still do that to a degree, as the weather reports are not always correct for our neck of the woods.

After reprimanding the religious people in this scripture from Matthew, Jesus warned his followers about the teachings of these leaders of the faith, who thought they were so wise, but couldn't recognize the signs of the times. Today, we still need to be wary of the teachings of religious leaders, cults, and even the media. If we read our Bibles regularly, we will recognize false teaching, but unfortunately there are many who blindly believe what is taught from every pulpit and TV documentary.

I remember when I was first trying to find God back in my early twenties. I visited a half dozen different types of churches, and felt very confused. They all claimed to be the "way", but they were all so different, and didn't always agree on things. So I decided to read the Bible for myself to figure it out. Which was difficult starting in Genesis. Nobody told me I should start with the gospels, and that this book was not like others that you read from cover to cover. I would encourage you to read the scriptures yourself to understand what God is saying, and be discerning about what teaching you sit under. This is exactly what Jesus was warning His followers to do.

Thank you Holy Spirit for guiding and directing our steps to the right sources for learning and growing in you. Amen

The Cosmos Praise Him

Every one of us is, in the cosmic perspective, precious. If a human disagrees with you, let him live. In a hundred billion galaxies, you will not find another. ~*Carl Sagan*

Psalm 89:5 TMT
God! Let the cosmos praise your wonderful ways, the
choir of holy angels sing anthems to your faithful ways!
Search high and low, scan skies and land, you'll find
nothing and no one quite like God.

I'm a big Star Trek fan. Our family used to have "Star Trek and Pizza" night on Saturdays. It's fun to imagine touring through space and finding all these different alien life forms, and see what it might look like to get to know them. I mean the universe is so BIG! There's got to be some kind of intelligent life out there, right? We sure do have wild imaginations, don't we? When God says he can do immeasurably more than we can ask or even imagine, I think, "I can imagine a lot, God!" (Eph 3:20)

The quote from Carl Sagan is quite sobering though. We can see so far out into space, and we know there are at least a hundred billion galaxies! And yet, where's the intelligent life? We aren't finding any. So what does that mean? It means that planet Earth and all the diverse life on it is very, very rare and special. Actually, according to the odds of evolution, it would have to be a miracle for life to randomly form on its own. Father God is the intelligent designer behind it all. Every created thing has his signature, and even the cosmos praise him. Yes, there is nothing and no one quite like God. Isn't it amazing that we can know the creator of the universe personally? That we are capable of feeling his love, and loving him back? That part feels like the real miracle to me.

Lord, I stand amazed by you and the power of your creative talents, but I am even more amazed that in the vastness of it all, you know me, and you love me. Thank you Father, for including me in your beautiful design. Thank you for quickening my spirit to know yours. Amen

Lights in the Sky

❧

The moon shines because its surface reflects light from the sun ~*livescience.com*

Genesis 1:14-15 NLT
Then God said, "Let lights appear in the sky to separate
the day from the night. Let them be signs to mark the
seasons, days, and years. Let these lights in the sky shine
down on the earth." And that is what happened.

I love nights with a full moon lighting up the forest outside my house. Sometimes the moon is in just the right position that it shines in the window right into my eyes, and wakes me up. I will sometimes get up and stand at the window a while, just gazing into the lighted evening. It always feels like a special time to meet with my Father, like maybe he just wanted to talk to me. I stand there struck by the quiet and beauty of the night, praising Papa God again for everything he's given me, then listen for prayer thoughts and promptings.

Recently, my daughter came to visit me from Alaska in mid-Spring, and we were really enjoying sitting outside in the warm sun. It does amaze me that the sun is light-years away, and yet so hot I can feel it's heat burning my skin. I'm so grateful for the heavenly lights God setup for planet Earth to give us light and heat and the seasons. Without them we would be in utter darkness, and there would be no life here.

Take a moment today to stand or sit in the sun and feel its warmth, and revive that childlike wonder in the perfection of creation and the lights in the sky that make it all possible. Try to catch a glimpse of the moon tonight and take a moment to listen for prayer promptings and that small voice of the Holy Spirit whispering, "hello my child".

Thank you Lord for your amazing design for the moon, the sun and the stars being perfectly set in place for life on planet Earth. Amen

Signs in the Heavens

God Himself uses heavenly phenomena as signs of
momentous events. ~ *Bibletools.org*

Matthew 2:8 TVT
And the star they had seen in the east guided them to Bethlehem. It went ahead of them and stopped over the place where the child was.

Today there are many trains of thought regarding the meanings of the stars. Years ago some of the New Age ideas were intriguing to me, but I found a different story about the stars in my Bible. It is a common trick of the enemy to disguise the truth to have us believe a lie. Anything to steer us away from finding Jesus, or having a deeper walk with our Father. Remember, we are in a spiritual battle after all.

God's Word speaks of signs in the heavens that are generally about important events, not our personalities, although there are certain scientific properties of celestial bodies that do effect our world, like how the full moon cycles effect the tides, how the path of stars mark seasons, and how the constellations guide sailors. There were signs in the heavens to announce the birth of Jesus, and also when He died on the cross. There will also be signs in the heavens when He returns. (See Matthew 24 and Revelation 6) Jesus told us to be looking for those signs, so we would not be taken by surprise. But we need to be wise about what we are looking for in the stars, and not be side tracked by the smoke and mirrors of modern culture. I think the important thing is to look to the source, the Word of God, for answers, and put our faith there. The deeper you dig into God's Word, the more answers you will find about these issues. The heavens speak of a Creator. Look deeper, and you can see his fingerprint in the skies.

Holy Spirit, thank you for giving me discernment about the signs in the heavens, and leading me to the truth. If there are lies, let them be exposed, and let your truths come shining through. Amen

Northern Lights

Aurora Borealis: an aurora that occurs in earth's northern hemisphere. ~*Merriam-Webster*

Job 26:7 & 13 NLT
He spreads out the northern skies over empty space; his Spirit made the heavens beautiful...

I've never seen the Aurora Borealis myself, but it fascinates me. It looks like a rift in the atmosphere that lets in a little bit of God's glory. I know there's a scientific explanation for it, but it looks like something out of heaven itself. It's so mysterious and beautiful, the way I suppose heaven will be. These beautiful phenomena give us pause in a hectic world to stop, look, and just take it in for a moment. Maybe these moments of beauty in the sky are the way the skies can praise him. Words are the realm of mankind, but this kind of beauty speaks volumes.

We need to intentionally look for moments of beauty in our days, and use these occasions to praise our Father for it. A moment of appreciation and praise elevates our soul and lifts our countenance to the giver of life. These moments sometimes bring a line of a song to mind, for example, A Thousand Hallelujahs: "Who else would rocks cry out to worship? Whose glory taught the stars to shine? Perhaps creation longs to have the words to sing, but this joy is mine. With a thousand hallelujahs, we magnify Your name, You alone deserve the glory, the honor and the praise. Lord Jesus, this song is forever Yours. A thousand hallelujahs, and a thousand more." You can listen and sing along online: https://youtu.be/U7XkZO07Jj0

Lord, thank you for those moments of spontaneous beauty in things created. I ask you to reveal more of them to me in my daily routine. Help me recognize them as a time to share a moment with you, and an opportunity to elevate my soul in the middle of my day. Amen

Skies Week Five Reflections and Journaling Points

Write your reflections of the readings from the last week.

<u>The Sign in the Sky:</u> *Surety about the end times.*

<u>The Cosmos Praise Him:</u> *Feel the Creator's love.*

<u>Lights in the Sky:</u> *Enjoying the light of the Sun and Moon.*

<u>Signs in the Heavens:</u> *Discerning the meaning of stars.*

<u>Northern Lights:</u> *Praise God and elevate your soul.*

<u>Other Reflections</u>

Skies
Week Six

The Bigger Picture

❧

Sometimes people lack the ability to see anything
that isn't right in front of them. *~Unknown*

Romans 1:20 NLT
For ever since the world was created, people have seen the
earth and sky. Through everything God made, they can
clearly see his invisible qualities—his eternal
power and divine nature. So they have
no excuse for not knowing God.

It's easy to get caught up in our own little worlds. We can get absorbed in our careers, our hobbies, our families and our busy lives, and never stop for a moment to look at the bigger picture around us. Sometimes it takes something big or drastic to cause us to pause and think beyond our own little worlds. Back in my early twenties, life got so hard and painful, that I found myself saying, "There must be more to life than this!" That was the beginning of my search for what I was missing.

They say everyone has a hole in their heart that only God can fill. Well, I didn't know about God, but it sure felt like life had to have some kind of purpose, and I was going to find mine. I wasn't interested in religion, and that whole train of thought, although I had an inkling that all the amazing beauty on planet Earth didn't just come out of some random accidental smashing of atoms. I could see how it all worked together, and that just didn't seem accidental or random at all. All the diversity on planet Earth sure seems special to me. I finally came around to see the bigger picture, and ignited my faith in the God of the universe.

This scripture makes it sound so simple and obvious, that everyone can clearly see, so we are without excuse. And yet the world struggles against it, just like I did, because we have tunnel vision, until the Lord opens our eyes to see the bigger picture. Then suddenly the light comes on. He is so patient, waiting for us to ask, and never pushing Himself on us. What a beautiful way to start a relationship.

Thank you Father for your grace and patience with me. Thank you for turning on the light so I could see and understand the bigger picture. Amen

Shadows in the Sky

A lunar eclipse is the shadow of earth on the moon.
Science facts: The moon makes a giant black spot that
appears to be the size of Australia, and it moves across
Earth's surface. *~Science Channel*

James 1:17 NLT
Whatever is good and perfect is a gift coming down
to us from God our Father, who created all the
lights in the heavens. He never changes or
casts a shifting shadow.

Watching the moon eclipse as it goes through the monthly cycle is pretty cool. Just think about how the planets are aligning every day in such a way that the earth casts its shadow on the moon to give us the familiar shapes of the moon we see in the night sky. Then when the earth is not aligned with the sun and moon, we get the full moon brilliance. But I didn't really think about how the moon also casts a shadow on the earth when it passes between the earth and the sun., like a big shadow without a cloud in the sky. I wonder if this is what happened the day Jesus died. The Bible says the sky grew dark for about three hours. It's interesting to think about shadows on a planetary scale!

James tells us that God never changes, or casts any shadows of doubt, so we can always rest assured that our God will always love us, and be there for us. This fact, above all else, is what comforts me the most in my journey through life as a Christian. To know that I'm never alone, and always have my Father to turn to. When there seems to be no one else that would listen or understand, my Jesus is there. I remember some days, before I knew Jesus, when I truly felt like I was all alone in the world. That no one cared about me. There's a difference in being lonely, and feeling all alone in the world. It's not something I would wish on any soul. It drives me to want to share this revelation of a loving spiritual Father with those that don't know he's there for them, because it's such a comfort to know the truth. Is there someone you can you share this comfort with today?

Papa God, thank you for always being there for us. Thank you that you don't change like shifting shadows. You're the same yesterday, today and forever. Hallelujah!

Sun Dogs

Sun dogs, with their characteristic mirroring of the sun's brilliance, frequently appear in pairs on either side of the sun, often within a halo. Caused by the refraction of the sun's rays passing through ice crystals in the atmosphere... ~Cochrane Eagle

Luke 7:46 NLT
You neglected the courtesy of olive oil to anoint my head, but she has anointed my feet with rare perfume.

Spotting a Sun Dog in the sky is a rare occasion. I've seen only a few in my lifetime, and it was always a special moment. They appear specific to an angle of the sun and the rare condition of ice crystals in the air, reflecting only to the person in the right place at the right time. If you get the opportunity to spot one, take a moment to enjoy it.

Luke tells a story about an event involving people being in the right place at the right time, with an uninvited guest. A prostitute in the house of a Pharisee was unheard of, but there she was, weeping and washing Jesus' feet with her hair and a rare perfume. Everyone there thought it was a disgusting scene, but Jesus used the moment as an object lesson. He knew the woman's sins were many, and she was so broken before him about it that she was pouring out her greatest possession as an offering. He said, "Her many sins have been forgiven, so she has shown me much love. But a person who is forgiven little, shows only little love." Then he told her, "Your faith has saved you; go in peace." This is what it looks like to be radically saved.

It resembles how I was radically saved, and why I love motorcycle ministry so much. I know that sometimes it just comes down to being at the right place at the right time (a divine appointment), to witness a rare event like "radical salvation". Someone who society would reject as unclean, can be saved and forgiven, still today.

Thank you Lord for this example of always giving second chances to even the most unholy people in the world. You love us all, and desire that we would all come to the saving knowledge of what Jesus did for them. Help me to see all people as those you love. Amen

Air Waves

Lenticular clouds are a visible sign of mountain waves in the air. Under certain conditions, long strings of lenticular clouds may form near the crest of each successive wave, creating a formation known as a wave cloud. ~*Wikipedia*

Ephesians 4:16 NLT
He makes the whole body fit together perfectly. As
each part does its own special work, it helps the
other parts grow, so that the whole body is
healthy and growing and full of love.

L enticular clouds are a special phenomena in the sky that you only see around mountains. I see them hovering over Mount Shasta from my kitchen window sometimes, and it looks like the mountain is wearing a little cloud hat. When conditions are just right, with wind flows and moisture, the clouds magically appear on site. It's interesting to think about how the mountain, the wind and the moisture all play a part to make something interesting and beautiful.

God made us as believers to work together the same way, as explained in Ephesians chapter 4. Each of us is unique and different, bringing our part to the table. Together we create something beautiful for the world to see: the Church. We all have a part to play for the whole body to be healthy and growing and full of love. Churches where the people are active and involved are full of life and love, and are a joy to be a part of. When the church is making a difference in the local community, it inspires and softens hearts of unbelievers that experience our joy as well. A group of believers that are united in spirit can not only change a community, they can change cities, and nations. A pastor recently shared, "Find out what God is doing, and be part of it." I also know that the Holy Spirit is looking for people with pure hearts ready to do his work. Have you asked the Lord how you can be a part of what he is doing in the world?

Holy Spirit, I ask you to quicken my mind and heart to see what my part is to help the other parts of the church grow. Give me the courage to get involved, and an anointing and passion to live for you. Amen

Unique Planets

uary 24, 2009 12:46UT   *Hubble Space Tel*

Hubble Heritage Team (STScI/AURA)

Saturn is the sixth planet from the Sun and the second-largest planet in our solar system. Adorned with thousands of beautiful ringlets, Saturn is unique among the planets. ~ *Solarsystem.nasa.gov*

Job 22:12 NLT
God is so great—higher than the heavens,
higher than the farthest stars.

Technology today is amazing. We can capture pictures of planets 900 million miles away! I read that Saturn takes twenty nine years to trek around the sun, but only 10.7 hours to rotate or spin around and call it a day. What a very creative God! Every planet is unique, every person is unique, and he calls them each by name. This universe is so amazing, it makes me wonder what comes next. What is Heaven like?

The word "Heaven" can be referred to as God's dwelling place (Psalm 103:19). Heaven can also mean the universe and its endless planets, stars and galaxies. (Psalm 8:3) The Bible gives us some clues, but we can only speculate. We do know that Jesus is there now preparing a place for us. I have pondered the idea that the new heaven and new earth might be a new place in the universe. Maybe another galaxy? We certainly are infatuated with the notion of space travel and exploring the universe. (Maybe I've watched a little too much Star Trek?) I believe our new home will be even more beautiful than Earth, and maybe we will be given jobs or responsibilities based on what we've been faithful with and preparing for in this life.

All we know is that we are foreigners here. Our real home is with our Jesus, and he's been preparing a place for us for 2000 years. I think we will be blown away by what we find. 1 Cor 2:9 says, "No eye has seen, no ear has heard, and no human mind has imagined what God has prepared for those who love him" These words give us hope for eternity.

Father, thank you for setting eternity in our hearts. Amen

Skies Week Six Reflections and Journaling Points

Write your reflections of the readings from the last week.

The Bigger Picture: *Seeing the light - what Jesus did for us.*

Shadows in the Sky: *We can always turn to our Father.*

Sun Dogs: *Anyone can be radically saved.*

Air Waves: *What is your part in the Church?*

Unique Planets: *What is heaven like?*

Other Reflections

Deserts
MEETING GOD IN THE DRY PLACES

Introduction

"...they looked toward the desert, and there was the glory of the Lord appearing in the cloud."
Exodus 16:10 NIV

If you've ever visited a desert place, you know the scorching sun beats down and the landscape seems barren and lifeless. We can sometimes find ourselves in a spiritual desert as well. It's easy to feel lost and alone in such a place, but it's often in these desert places that we experience God's presence in a profound and life-changing way.

They say a spiritual desert can be a place of great testing and refinement, where we are forced to rely on God in a deeper way than ever before. It can also be a place of revelation, where we can see God's hand at work, even if it is sometimes only evident in retrospect.

But as we journey through our deserts, we can find hope and strength in God's promises. Even in the middle of our trials, God is at work, helping us to let go of the old, bring in new life and build up our character.

In my childhood, I spent some years growing up in the California desert. Then more recently, I lived in the Arizona desert. I have some first hand experience of how the desert can take the physical life out of you. I've also experienced the beauty of a desert in full super bloom that takes your breath away. Every place God created has it's own kind of beauty.

I share some of my life stories in this book. Some will inspire wonder in the creation, reminding us what an awesome God we serve. Other stories hit closer to the heart and remind us how to find comfort in the precious Holy Spirit, and how much we need him.

My hope is that these pages will help you take comfort in knowing that even in the driest, most desolate places, God is with you, leading you to new growth and life, and showing us the beauty that is right in front of us.

May the Lord bless you through this journey. ~Author

Deserts
Week One

Red Rocks

I'll never forget it. I was starting to hike up the red rocks, and honestly, it was as if I heard the rock say, "You have the answers. You are your teacher." I thought I was having an auditory hallucination. ~*Gwyneth Paltrow*

Isaiah 61:3 NIV
...to bestow on them a crown of beauty instead of ashes,
the oil of joy instead of mourning, and a garment of praise
instead of a spirit of despair.

The red rocks of Sedona are one of the most beautiful desert places in the world. These kind of landscapes make you wonder how they came to be. I believe the Lord gave us this amazing scenery just for the beauty of it!

When I lived in Arizona, I made many trips to Sedona. It was usually full of tourists, but the beauty of the rocks kept drawing me back. The colorful layers and towering spires always had me dropping my jaw at the beauty of the area. The wonder of this place was revealed out of the chaos of events in the far past. Beauty for ashes. That's what God does.

Time spent in nature is always great therapy, and pushes away the pressures and heaviness of life. You may not be able to visit the red rocks, but any place in nature that makes you smile and relax will do.

Sometimes, in our desert moments, it can feel like we are in a low place. But it's in those places that we can hear the voice of God speaking to us louder. Why? Because we are listening. We listen better when our lowliness presses in and all we can do is look up.

As you journey through the deserts of your life, remind yourself of his presence in all things, and get lost in the possibilities of what beauty he will bring about out of your chaos. He always has a plan, and works everything out for our good.

Thank you Father for bringing the beauty out of my ashes. Thank you for hearing me and guiding me when my spirit is in a desert place. Amen

Frozen Desert

We were marooned in a frozen desert. There was not a
sign of life on the horizon and a thousand signs of
death... The marvel is we did not all die of cold.
~Wilfred Owen

Psalm 29:8 NIV
The voice of the Lord shakes the desert;
the Lord shakes the Desert of Kadesh.

Deserts are usually known for their scorching heat and relentless sun, but in some regions or seasons, they can be bitterly cold as well. I remember a road trip I took as a young adult, where I saw a snow covered desert for the first time. I was in awe. Another aha moment in discovering something new about planet Earth! At that time I had no idea you could freeze in the desert. I was truly surprised.

Physical cold is one thing, but a frozen heart can take the warmth out of living. Sometimes hurtful experiences can make us grow cold toward others and life in general. It can be hard to overcome those feelings. This is where forgiveness can set us free. It may sound simplistic, but I truly believe the only way to get past deep hurts is to dig them up from the deep and bring them to our Jesus. These kind of wounds are exactly what he came to heal.

Maybe you are one of the lucky ones that has had a sweet life surrounded by love. I'm truly happy for you, and I hope you never have to feel the pain of a cold heart. Maybe you know someone who is hurting this way that you can help with this message. When we are in these cold places, we need to be real for a moment and face our baggage so we can let it go, even if it involves forgiveness. The Word says to bring all our cares to him, because he cares for us. We can trust God to replace our hurts with grace and love. It's so worth it.

Father, I invite the warmth of your love to pour into the cold parts of my heart. Help me to surrender these areas to you; even the deep buried hurts. Give me the grace to forgive. Amen (Read this prayer a few times, if you need to.)

Super Bloom

A flower blooming in the desert proves to the world that
adversity, no matter how great, can be overcome.
~ Matshona Dhliwayo

Isaiah 35:1
The desert and the parched land will be glad; the
wilderness will rejoice and blossom. Like the crocus,
it will burst into bloom; it will rejoice greatly
and shout for joy!

What an amazing sight it is to see the desert in super bloom. It only happens about every ten to fifteen years, so if you get to see the phenomenon, it's a rare and special sight. Imagine taking a walk through God's colorful garden of splendor in the desert sands. A place that you expect to be dry and dead is completely transformed and is now full of life and color. It's a picture of what he can do in our lives.

Today's scripture talks about a desert in super bloom, rejoicing greatly and shouting for joy! When was the last time you did that? We can all use more joy in our lives, right? If you haven't felt real joy lately, I speak that over you now. You can speak it over yourself by reading Isaiah 35:1 and applying it to yourself. You are the desert that will be glad. You will rejoice and blossom. You will burst into bloom and rejoice greatly! Are you feeling it yet? I challenge you to pray and speak this over yourself all day today (or longer), and see if you don't begin to feel real hope and joy creeping in. Make this one of your mantra verses that you go to - especially in the dark times - to remember that God is bringing your transformation. He's preparing your time to rejoice and shout for joy. Yes and amen!

Lord thank you for giving us the vision of transformation and joy coming to the dry desert places of our hearts. Help me to see it ahead, and begin to rejoice even before it arrives. Amen

Sea of Sand

The desert is so huge, and the horizon so distant, that
they make a person feel small, and as if he should
remain silent. ~ *Paulo Coelho*

Isaiah 41:10 NIV
Do not fear, for I am with you; do not be
dismayed, for I am your God.

The desert is a place of extremes. It can be hot and dry during the day, and cold and desolate at night. It's a place where life seems scarce, and the landscape can seem barren and lifeless. But in the midst of this harsh environment, there is beauty to be found, and lessons to be learned about God's faithfulness.

In the Bible, we read about many desert experiences. The Israelites wandered in the desert for forty years, learning to trust in God's provision and guidance. Elijah fled to the desert, where he was fed by ravens and experienced God's presence in a still, small voice. And Jesus was led into the desert, where he was tempted by the devil, but ultimately relied on God's word to overcome.

The desert times of our life can be a place of spiritual growth, where we learn to trust God to provide and give us strength. It's a place where we can find a deeper faith, and where we can discover the value in the challenges we face. Believe this, and your battle is already won.

If you find yourself in a desert place, remember that God is with you. Someone once told me that we become what we focus on. If we focus on what we don't have, we live from a place of lack. But God has given us everything we need if we steward well what we do have. Today, bring your focus back to what God has already given you. If the vastness of your desert makes you feel small, just remember how big our God is.

My Jesus, thank you for being with me in the dry places. Please help me to rely on you more for strength and guidance. Teach me how to grow closer to you and be a good steward of what you have already given me. Amen

Sand Storms

The storms of life can make you better, or bitter.
~D.K. Olukoya

Habakkuk 1:9 NIV
Their hordes advance like a desert wind and
gather prisoners like sand.

A desert sand storm is a freak of nature. Named "Haboob" in the Sudan Arabian desert, it is a weather phenomenon that is a rather scary event.

I encountered a haboob in the Arizona desert some years ago as I was driving home from a road trip. I saw a wall of swirling sand ahead and pulled over immediately. What the heck? I'd never seen anything like it. Then I realized with sudden terror that it was coming toward me fast, and there was going to be no escape. I figured the only thing to do was to stay put and hope for the best. As the storm cloud engulfed me and my car, flying things were coming from out of no where, beating up my car... sticks, cactus, car parts! I was just hoping the wind wasn't strong enough to pick my car up and throw me around! After about twenty excruciating minutes and steady prayers, the storm passed. I was shook up, but also thrilled that I had just been through an extraordinary experience and lived to tell about it.

Life can throw us some curve balls, can't it? We can suddenly find ourselves in bad situations, with seemingly nothing we can do about it but pray. When there's no way out, we must go through, and praying for God's protection and guidance is the smartest thing we can do in these times. It's normal to feel a little fearful when things are out of our control, and it's not easy to push all that aside and trust God. But each time we do that, it gets easier. There is no scary thing on planet Earth that he doesn't know about. He will get us through it, and maybe even give us a story to tell others.

Has the Lord given you a story that someone else needs to hear to help them trust God in their situation?

Papa God, thank you for always being there for me to turn to in the scary times. Help me to trust you through every scary situation. Help me to learn the lessons and comfort others with the comfort you've given me. Amen

Deserts Week One Reflections and Journaling Points

Write your reflections of the readings from the last week.

Red Rocks: Thank him for giving you beauty for ashes.

Freezing Desert: Giving God our hurts and forgiving.

Super Bloom: Thank God for the coming transformation.

Sea of Sand: Being thankful he is with you in the dry places.

Sand Storms: How has God gotten you through a storm?

Other Reflections

Deserts
Week Two

Desert Beauty

The desert tells a different story every time one ventures
into it. ~ *Robert Edison Fulton Jr*

Isaiah 33:17 NIV
Your eyes will see the king in his beauty and
view a land that stretches afar.

The desert can be a challenging and harsh environment, with its intense heat, dryness, and rugged terrain, and yet life in the desert has learned to adapt and thrive in these hard conditions.

I have to say the desert fascinates me. When I was young and too busy to notice it, I would rush past the desert in an effort to just get through it on my travels. But if you stop and sit in the desert for a spell, you might be mesmerized by the simple beauty it offers. One of the things I love about it is that it's so empty and vast. No noise, no people, and the long views with nothing but wilderness. I enjoy the quietness of the desert. This is where I can really connect with our Father.

In many ways, the desert can be a metaphor for our own lives - full of challenges and adversity, but also full of potential and beauty. We will always have to deal with the challenges, but I try not to give it my full attention. Life can be full of beauty depending on what we focus on.

When I am in a dry spiritual place, I ask the Lord, "What do you want me to learn here?" I try to find quiet time to listen, but I don't always get answers. Many times the lessons aren't seen until further down the road. But we trust.

Getting close to nature is my favorite place to reflect on issues that are going on, and talk to Papa about it. Sometimes we might need to learn how to adapt, rather than hold out for that 'someday' when things will change or get back to normal. What if things will never get back to normal? What if this is the new normal? Can we look for the beauty here and now?

When it seems like life is too heavy, I purposefully look for beauty to redirect my focus. Could you use some time in nature to help you find the beauty in your day to day living?

Father, help me to find the beauty in every part of my life, especially in the challenges. Amen.

Desert Mountains

God moves mountains that we don't see.
~ *Guideposts Magazine*

1 Cor 13:2 NIV
...and if I have a faith that can move mountains,
but do not have love, I am nothing.

The desert is home to some of the most rugged and beautiful mountain ranges in the world. The desert mountains show us their layers and structure like no other mountains can. They look like solid rock, strong and immovable. Was God talking about spiritual things when he said our faith could move mountains?

I've had my share of mountains standing in the way of my progress. I remember a time when I was trying to buy my dream house, and everything seemed to be going along fine, until a past credit issue stopped everything in its tracks. It seemed like an immovable mountain, and I prayed passionately for God to move it for me. Finally, a new lender accepted my application and the deal went through. Thank you Lord! I know that I received my own little miracle that day.

If you're staring down a big mountain in your life, remember that God is like the solid rock mountain in the desert that we can turn to, and that he is still in the business of doing miracles. Our scripture today tells us that our faith in God's power can move our mountains. But don't forget the part about having love, or all those miracles mean nothing.

Maybe the whole point of this passage is to remind us to be loving toward others. How do we treat others in the middle of our obstacles? Are we serving others or just being self-serving in those times? Remember Solomon's prayer when God said he could have anything? He wanted wisdom to serve the people. Now there's an example of selfless love.

Thank you Lord, for the strong mountains that point to your power, and the lesson on how love means serving others. Amen

Coyotes

Coyote is always out there waiting, and coyote is always hungry. ~ *Navajo (Diné) proverb*

Ecclesiastes 9:4 NLT
There is hope only for the living. As they say, "It's better to
be a live dog than a dead lion!"

There are valuable lessons to be learned from the coyotes of the desert. They live in a harsh and unforgiving place, but have adapted in their own unique way to the challenges of the arid landscape. These desert animals can teach us about perseverance, adaptability, and being survivors.

Sometimes we need all those things, don't we? I had a job in my twenties that really challenged me, with a boss that was unbelievably difficult. Some days I would lock my office door and just cry and pray for a way out. I wanted to walk out so many times, but my pastor had been teaching about having integrity, and I knew this was my test. So I bit my lip and persevered, while I started a new job search. After several interviews, I was confused about which job offer to take. My friend ask me, "If you could have any job you wanted, what would it be? Let's not limit God!" Long story short, my dream job was to work for myself, and God opened the doors for me to start my own business. He even used my old boss to endorse me and send me my first customer! What an awesome God we serve! I believe he honored me for taking the high road and doing the right thing.

That's how we act like the coyote - we do what we must to survive, with integrity. We do our part, and God does his part, and it all works together to bring us to a better place in the end.

I love You Lord, for teaching me the lessons that lead to blessings and rewards. Some lessons are hard, but I know they build character, and I'm so grateful you love me enough to make me more like you. Amen

Desert Night Sky

The desert, when the sun comes up. I couldn't tell
where heaven stopped and the Earth began.
~ *Tom Hanks*

Song of Solomon 6:10
"Who is this, arising like the dawn, as fair as the moon, as bright as the sun, as majestic as an army with billowing banners?"

The desert is known for its wide-open spaces and rugged landscapes, but it is also home to some of the most stunning night skies on earth. When the sun sets and the stars come out, the desert sky displays the vastness of the universe like no where else. It's a place to marvel at His creation.

When I was in my twenties, I would drive out to the desert over a weekend just to spend the night under the stars. I remember a time when my younger sister and I drove out to the desert, about a hundred miles from our home town. We found a dirt road to drive down until we could get beyond any city lights or sounds of the freeway so we could see the night sky better. We took our sleeping bags and climbed out on the hood of my old '55 Oldsmobile, and lay back on the windshield to see how many shooting stars we could see. We could have stayed out there all night, but when we heard the coyotes start to howl, we decided to sleep in the car - windows up and the doors locked!

Looking out into the universe at night makes me feel very small and insignificant for sure. It's amazing to think about how small planet Earth really is in the grand scheme of things. And then we are only one person in eight billion people living here. Think about how special we are to be alive on this planet, when as far as we can see into the universe, we are the only place with life out there. Looking at the stars helps me to put my problems into perspective, and makes it easier to let things go that really aren't that important after all.

Thank you Father for showing us how big you really are by looking out into the universe. Help us to not take ourselves and our little problems so seriously. Amen

The Saguaro

Being negative only makes a difficult journey more difficult. You may be given a cactus, but you don't have to sit on it. ~*Joyce Meyer*

2 Samuel 22:17-18 NIV
...thorns had come up everywhere, the ground was covered with weeds, and the stone wall was in ruins.

The Saguaro cactus is a protected species of cactus in Arizona. They transplant them when building roads in an effort to save them. I found them intriguing to look at. Each one different from the next.

The cactus may be looked upon by many in a negative way, because they are full of thorns and live in a hot, dry desert. But I've learned some interesting and positive facts about the Saguaro. In late Spring, they bloom pretty little white flowers on the tips of every arm. Later, the flowers die off and make sweet red fruit. Native Americans used to gather the fruit, and it has a wonderful sweet/tart flavor. The taste is like a cross between a kiwi and a strawberry.

I went on a Saguaro fruit gathering mission one year. I brought a fifteen foot long PVC stick with me to knock them off the top, but Saguaros are two to three times that tall! I had to find some growing on a hill and climb on rocks to get high enough to knock off a few fruit hoping I wouldn't fall into them. It was a prickly adventure, and I made some cactus apple fruit leather that my friends and family got to experience as Christmas gifts that year.

So what is the lesson here? There is always something positive to find in every ugly situation. We can take a clue from the quote and the scripture today. If we stay in that harsh negative place, thorns will come up and weeds start growing in our hearts. Eventually, our life is in ruins. There is power in positive thinking and looking for the good in things.

Father, help us to find the beauty and a positive thing about every thorny situation in our lives. Amen

Deserts Week Two Reflections and Journaling Points

<u>*Desert Beauty:*</u> *Finding the beauty in day to day living.*

<u>*Desert Mountains:*</u> *Moving mountains with Love.*

<u>*The Coyotes:*</u> *Surviving with integrity.*

<u>*Desert Night Skies:*</u> *How big is our God, and how small we are.*

<u>*The Saguaro:*</u> *A positive outlook to a thorny situation.*

<u>*Other Reflections*</u>

Week Three

Desert Sunset

Peace is seeing a sunset and knowing who to thank.
~Amish Proverb

Psalm 19:1 NIV
The heavens declare the glory of God; the skies proclaim
the work of his hands.

Sunsets are a stunning display of God's handiwork, and they seem especially colorful in the desert. Watching the colors of the sky slowly shift from gray and white, into pink and orange is one of my favorite things to do. It feels very peaceful, like the skies are bringing the issues of the day to a sweet end, leaving us with a bit of beauty to cap it off, and helping us to let go of any lingering heaviness.

Wouldn't it be wonderful if we could do that at the end of every day? What if we were to let go of any heaviness and just rest in another completed day? Can we be satisfied that we did the best we could, and let ourselves relax in knowing what ever we left undone, will be there for us tomorrow? I know from personal experience, that is not always what happens. I sometimes hold on to things into the night, and it keeps me awake. But the Word tells us, "Do not worry. Learn to pray about everything. Give thanks to God as you ask him for what you need." (Phil 4:6 NLT)

We can't always catch a sunset to help us let go of the day, but we can use the Philippians verse above as a prayer to give the concerns of each day to him so we can stop worrying, and end our day in a restful peace, knowing that what ever we left undone is in his hands. We might need to lean back into things in the morning, but for now, it's ok to let go. The ultimate bedtime prayer to end our days.

Papa God, thank you for always being there to take on our worries and concerns as we remember to pray about everything, and ask you for what we need. Amen

Balancing Rocks

This was rad to see! So many cool rocks! ~
Unknown Traveler

Song of Songs 8:5 NLT
Who is this coming up from the desert, resting on her loved one?"

The photo today is from Marble Canyon - a place I visited a few times in Arizona. There are all these amazing balancing rocks scattered around the landscape that have you scratching your head wondering how they happened, and how they stay there without toppling over.

Our lives are sometimes a balancing act as we go through each day, aren't they? Our modern society packs more and more on our plates, and if we're honest, we may be guilty of overloading ourselves, because we want to do it all, and we say, "I've got this!" But then we find out it's not as easy as we thought, and it's created stress. We might need to take a thing or two off of our plates to create more margin in our lives.

I love this bit of scripture from Song of Songs today, that gives us a picture of a young girl coming up out of the desert with complete confidence in where she is at in this place and time in her life, because she is resting on her beloved . For us, that is the Lord.

If you feel like your life is out of balance, let this scripture give you a vision for something different. Picture yourself walking out of your desert with complete confidence as you rest in the Lord. If you need to take some action to create that margin, then give it some prayer and let go with confidence, knowing that you will be able to enter into that sweet rest with your Father.

Papa God, please keep pouring out your Spirit of wisdom on me to know what to keep and what to take off my plate to reduce stress and walk in your rest. Amen

Loneliest Road

Sometimes the road ahead is just a line to the horizon that doesn't care if we run out of gas and reminds us that we are tiny traveling blips in the vast macrocosm of the universe. That's pretty much what it's like to drive Highway 50 through Nevada.
~ *Article from TimeOut.com*

Psalms 62:1-2 NLT
My soul is quiet and waits for God alone. He is the One who
saves me. He alone is my rock and the One who saves me. He is
my strong place. I will not be shaken.

Sometimes the road we are on can feel pretty lonely, and seem to go on forever. There is a road in the desert going from California through Nevada that is called the 'loneliest road' because it stretches for miles and miles without a stop and no signs of human life. I've driven this and others like it myself, and after a while they can make one start to feel desperate to see some sign of life. The impending doom of getting stuck in a desert with no help in sight becomes real.

When we find ourselves in a spiritual and emotional place of loneliness, with seemingly no one to turn to, there is Psalm 62. This small passage in the Bible packs power. If you meditate on these words, it begins to sink into your spirit that you are not really alone. Papa God is there. He is our rock. He is the One that will save us. He is our strong place to run to. He is always guiding us and protecting us through this journey called "life".

Sometimes it's just the act of crying out to God that releases the anxiety and fears, and brings us relief. Letting the tears flow and absorbing the promises of his word will bring us to a better place. There is always an exchange in seeking God. When we give our hurts to him, we let those be replaced by his love, which gives us new hope and confidence to move forward from a better frame of mind.

Do you need to make an exchange with God today? His love for your hurts and fears?

Papa God, thank you for being there for me and offering me such a great exchange. Help me to make my offerings and receive your gifts and promises. Amen

Roadrunners

Roadrunner teaches how to find the hidden humor in situations all while showing you the path to greater productivity and efficiency. ~ *Roadrunner Symbolism*

Luke 13:19 NLT
It is like a mustard seed, which a man took and planted in his garden. It grew and became a tree, and the birds perched in its branches.

Everything in God's creation has potential to be so much more than ordinary. Bugs aren't just bugs; butterflies have beauty that move us. Birds aren't just birds; they take flight and we marvel to watch them master the air. Creation was for God's pleasure, but I think he knew it would fill us with wonder.

The roadrunner is definitely a very unique bird to study, and I personally find joy when getting glimpses of them, which is a fairly rare occasion. It's interesting that we have a habit of assigning symbolism to animals that make them much more significant than just a simple creature. God gave us eyes in our hearts and souls that see beyond the ordinary.

In our modern society we can sometimes feel insignificant, but we need to remember that in all of the extraordinary elements of creation, we are actually his masterpiece. And even in our day to day routines, we can do extraordinary things. For example, the scripture today mentions the simple act of planting a seed. A seed planted in the ground may produce a tree that birds can call home. Planting a seed in someone's heart, can change their life forever. Just watch what happens when you find something extraordinary about a person in your day today, and tell them about how special they are. Plant a seed of joy, and ask the Lord to water it. I hope God continues to reveal what is special about you too!

Papa God, thank you for so much beauty and potential you display all around us. Help us to see the gifts you give each one of us that make us special and unique. May we shine a light on what makes others special too. Amen

Mesquite Trees

Leave it alone, mi amor. It's in the tree's
nature to be stubborn. It's a survivor."
~ *Guadalupe Garcia McCall, Under the Mesquite*

Jeremiah 17:7-8 (NIV)
But blessed is the one who trusts in the Lord, whose confidence
is in him. They will be like a tree planted by the water that
sends out its roots by the stream. It does not fear when heat
comes; its leaves are always green. It has no worries in a year
of drought and never fails to bear fruit.

The mesquite tree is a remarkable symbol of resilience, thriving in the hot and dry conditions of the desert. The mesquite tree's secret is that it draws its strength from deep roots that reach the moisture far beneath the earth.

Like the mesquite tree, we can draw strength and resilience from our faith and trust in God. With his help, we can endure the most difficult circumstances and come out stronger on the other side. This is why we must let our roots in the Lord grow deep and strong.

I think about how the strength of the mesquite tree not only helps itself, but provides resources to others as well. Its shade can save a life for anyone lost in the desert. The bean pods are edible, and the wood has a special fragrance and quality sought after for special purposes.

When we are strong in the Lord, it not only helps us in the hard times, but we become a beacon of hope for others. We can be the shelter they can rest in, and our lives become an example that shows there is still hope. There is always hope. Because of our strength and confidence, others can stand tall and strong. Is there someone you can offer strength to today?

Thank you Father for lessons we can learn from the tree that survives with its strong, deep roots. What a blessing to be able to use the strength you give me, to strengthen others. Help me to keep growing my roots deeper in you. Amen

Deserts Week Three Reflections and Journaling Points

Desert Sunsets: Ending our day in a restful peace.

Balancing Rocks: Walking out of our deserts with confidence.

Loneliest Road: Exchanging our hurts for his love..

Roadrunners: Finding extraordinary things about ourselves.

Mesquite Tree: Become strong to be a blessing to others.

Other Reflections

Deserts
Week Four

Palm Tree Oasis

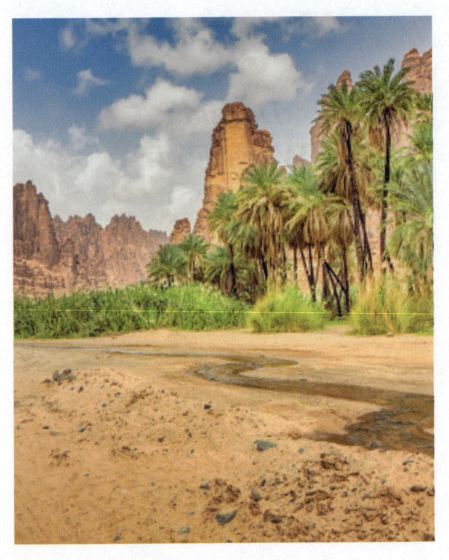

Wild and free, just like a palm tree.
~ *laurewanders.com*

Psalm 92:12-14 NIV
The righteous flourish like the palm tree and grow like a cedar
in Lebanon. They are planted in the house of the Lord; they
flourish in the courts of our God. They still bear fruit in old age;
they are ever full of sap and green.

The palm tree is a majestic and steadfast pillar in the desert, standing tall and unyielding in the harsh landscape. A true symbol of the desert oasis, these trees are like a life line of salvation. We know they are a sign that there will be water and relief from the sun.

The strength of the palm tree in the desert, is its ability to bend and not break, even in hurricane force winds. They can weather any storm, and survive the baking heat.

How can we dig into this kind of strength? Some days, we wonder, is it in us? Although we might not be able to handle real physical storms, our scripture today reminds us that we can flourish like the palm tree in our own worlds. Even in old age, we can expect to bear fruit and be full of life. Why? Because we are God's righteous people who have been planted in the house of the Lord! Our lives represent a desert oasis to the world, revealing the promises of God by our very existence. We hold out the hope of life to those who are lost. Our answer lies in serving others.

The world is a harsh place, and there are so many that need a refuge, even if they don't know what that looks like. What a difference we can make if we see ourselves as the palm tree of the Lord, planted to bring light and hope to others. Is there a thirsty soul you can show the way to the refreshing waters?

Papa God, I am amazed at how you see us and have set us apart to do a special work in the Earth. Help us to step into our role as your oasis in the desert. Amen

Cactus Flowers

The flower that blooms in adversity is the most beautiful of all. ~*Jooinn*

The flowers are springing up, the season of singing birds has come, and the cooing of turtledoves fills the air.

T here is something special about cactus blooms. Maybe because of the environment they live in, their color and beauty seems to be magnified. Even in the bleakest conditions on planet Earth, life and beauty can be found.

Have you ever heard the saying, "We were born for such a time as this?" The thinking behind it, is that we were born into adversity, on purpose. As if what we have to offer was designed to fit exactly into what is needed most right now, in the time that we live in. The cactus blooms stick out in the desert landscape as something special to be noticed and appreciated. What if God put us into our landscape to stand out as something special?

Sometimes it's hard to see ourselves as 'special', and yet each of us are unique. A mentor recently told me that we need to be authentic and uniquely ourselves in this world. To do anything else (trying to be like someone else, or think that we aren't good enough because we aren't like others) is an insult to the God who made us. We have a place in this world, and a purpose to fulfill that no one other than us can do. That really freed me, because when I think about it, I've spent a lot of energy over the years trying to become what I thought was the 'status quo'.

This is not like the thinking some have about being different on purpose. How about we start being free to be who God made us to be, and honor that by being authentic?

Papa God, thank you for making me unique and special. I don't want to pretend to be someone I'm not. Help me to be authentically who you made me to be. Amen

Ancient Desert Fortress

King Herod's ancient fortress in Masada.

Matthew 2:7 NLT
Then Herod called for a private meeting with the
wise men, and he learned from them the time
when the star first appeared.

It is said that Herod built this fortress only a couple decades before the birth of Jesus, for protection. Then when the ancient Romans overtook Judea in the first century A.D., the grounds became a fortress for the Jewish people.

Was this the place where Herod heard about a Messiah being born, and talked to the wise men who were seeking the baby? He wanted to get intel so he could vanquish the rumor of a coming king. But history shows that Herod died before Jesus started his ministry, and his fortress didn't save him. In fact the Jewish people obtained the property after he was gone. How's that for poetic justice?

It's interesting to think about this landscape around Jesus' birth. Bethlehem is part of the Judean desert. It looks so inhospitable, and yet God was working out his plan of the ages there. Can anything good come out of the dry desert? That's a big YES. The miracle birth of Christ.

Are you in a desert that you feel nothing good can come out of? Maybe you need to think again. Is God working out the plan of your life while you wait in the desert? Is he thinking about your miracle? Something I learned recently, is that "things don't happen to us, they happen for us." If we look at our deserts like that, we begin to have anticipation for amazing things ahead. God is working all things together.

Father thank you for the places that bring scripture to life. Thank you for miracles in the desert. Thank you for my desert, and my miracle! Amen

Desert Waves

The Vermilion Cliffs National Monument has some of the
most visually striking geologic sandstone.

Ezekiel 43:2 NLT
The sound of his coming was like the roar of rushing waters,
and the whole landscape shone with his glory.

So much of the most phenomenal landscapes and geologic formations on planet Earth were clearly the direct result of a LOT of water (a global flood maybe?) rushing through and leaving its mark. Most scientists won't agree to that statement, and you may have another explanation, but what my eyes see, seem to line up with scripture. In an effort to minimize any spiritual accountability, the world strives to find another answer. I was once in that pool, but have since found that my faith doesn't need to have all the answers to simply believe.

In 1st Peter 1:17 we read, *"These trials will show that your faith is genuine. It is being tested as fire tests and purifies gold—though your faith is far more precious than mere gold."*

It's a hard fact, but our bible teaches that our faith will be tested, through our mistakes and through our trials. Someone recently said to me, "What if there are no mistakes? What if there are only lessons? And lessons may be taught again and again until they are learned." This reminds me that sometimes the lesson is to trust even if I don't have all the answers. We don't need to stress about figuring everything out. We may never understand why our spouse does certain things, or be able to change it. But we need to accept and love them anyway. We may never understand why we didn't get that promotion, but we need to serve the team leader well anyway. I may not sell a million books, but God wants me to write it anyway!

Our faith is far more precious than mere gold. We may not know the value of it until we pass over to be with our Lord, but it's enough for me to know I can trust the process. You can trust the process too.

Thank you Father for that inner peace to know it is well with my soul, and that I can trust you even though I don't have all the answers. Amen

Rare Beauty

Antique Arizona postcard with two kinds of saguaro.

Luke 7:46
You neglected the courtesy of olive oil to anoint my head, but she has anointed my feet with rare perfume.

Crested Saguaros have an unusual mutation resulting in the growth of large fan-shaped crests at the end of a saguaro's main stem and arms. Something went wrong with the DNA of the cactus while it was growing, and it got a little creative! Scientists have tried to pin down what causes this recurring phenomenon, but so far have not been able to. I wonder if it's a long lost strain of cactus that occasionally shows itself. Either way, it's a rare and beautiful scene. It's estimated to only occur once out of every 200,000 cactus.

Rare things always peak our interest, especially if they are a real anomaly. I think we love to experience something new that we've never encountered before. Also, rare things have more value.

They say that it may take a Saguaro cactus about seventy five years before it grows its first arm. They grow very slowly, only about one and a half inches in it's first eight years! So the crested saguaro might be hundreds of years old before they bloom.

Some of us make the mistake of thinking we are too old to make a difference or add any beauty to the world. Not true! We might not have as much energy as we did when we were younger, but we have so much learned wisdom to offer the world. I plan on being a rare bird and blossom in my latter years. How about you? It's never too late, my friend.

Papa God, thank you for glimpses of rare beauty to inspire and encourage us to give away what you have given us to a world that needs your wisdom; something that is becoming more and more rare to find. Amen

Deserts Week Four Reflections and Journaling Points

Palm Tree Oasis: How can we be an oasis to a thirsty world?

Cactus Flowers: Being authentically who God made me to be..

Ancient Fortresses: Thanking God for our desert miracle.

Desert Waves: Trust. We don't have to understand everything.

Rare Beauty: How can we blossom in rare and beautiful ways?

Other Reflections

Deserts
Week Five

Slot Canyons

Water paths sculpted the red rocks into a piece of art.

Psalm 119:35 TPT
Guide me on the paths that please you.

Antelope Canyon in the Arizona desert is a long and twisty slot canyon. As you walk through, the path gets skinnier, until at one point it's a real squeeze to get through. These tight canyons were made by flash floods that came through cracks in the rocks with a bit of force. This canyon still gets flooded during a monsoon season, so the water and sands are still carving and smoothing the canyon walls. The Native Americans who own the land, won't allow anyone to visit the canyon when rain threatens for this reason. It can be a dangerous path.

As believers, we walk a different path than the world. The world doesn't understand why we follow a God they can't see, or how we can trust, when sometimes, our paths lead us into hard times. Yes, desert seasons are not easy for anyone, but have you considered that it may be required sometimes to get us back on the right path?

Personally, there have been times I've felt like I've been in a 'rut' or otherwise stuck without knowing what path to take. When we ask our Father to guide us on the paths that please him, we can't go wrong. It may not be an instant fix, but I believe he begins working things together to show us a better way. When we can speak the Word over our issues, it can't come back to him without accomplishing what he sent it out to do. (See Isaiah 55:11)

The truth is, our Father gives us the power to make our own choices in life, and we can certainly get ourselves into trouble - what parent couldn't say that about their child? But thank God for this verse! We can ask him to redirect our steps toward the path that pleases him. This is the first step in the right direction.

Papa God, thank you for being there to turn to when we find ourselves on the wrong path. Thank you for helping us adjust our sails to return to paths that please you. Amen

Death Valley

We drove through the Mojave Desert, Owens Valley and Death Valley, and the dust entered our bloodstream and flowed through to every part of our body. ~Karl Wiggins

Deut 32:9 NLT
He found them in a desert land, in an empty, howling wasteland. He surrounded them and watched over them; he guarded them as he would guard his own eyes.

I recently took a trip to visit Death Valley and spent a few days there to get some inspiration for this book. As God would have it, I was experiencing my own little 'desert trial' at the time. So when I asked him what lessons he would teach us in the deepest, driest, hottest desert, I was all ears.

One of the things Holy Spirit showed me there, was that the physical desert can kill us if we stay too long, and we aren't prepared, or if we don't do something to get ourselves out. Too long in a spiritual desert, can break our spirits too.

I was reminded that when we are talking about desert seasons, sometimes these dead zones want to draw us into depression, and we can get stuck. I think what the Spirit was saying, is "don't give up." Maybe a better way to say it is, "don't give in to it." Fight it every time! But if you are in a time of depression, don't stay there. Fight your way out. Remember that Jesus died for your freedom!

I believe we have these trials so that when harder things come, we won't be shaken. Paul says that no discipline is easy when we are going through it, but in the end we are stronger. Paul even said that it was a great honor for him to go through tests and trials, because the Lord deemed him worthy to be tested and used that way. Did we sign up for this? Yes, when we surrendered our lives to God, we asked him to come in. He's never going to leave us the same, and will be making us more like Jesus every day.

Our scripture today tells the story of God watching over his people in the desert and guarding them. Notice that he didn't take them out of the desert, but he helped them get through it. He hasn't gone anywhere. He's there to help us get through our deserts too.

Lord, help me to trust you to get me through my deserts, and to be looking for the lessons to be learned. Amen

Bare Mountains

The hardest mountain to climb is the one within.
J. Lynn

1 Cor 14:25 NIV
...as the secrets of their hearts are laid bare. So they
will fall down and worship God, exclaiming,
"God is really among you!"

In the depths of Death Valley you can't help noticing that the mountains are completely naked and bare, with all their layers and scars out in the open to plainly see. Nothing hidden.

When I was visiting the area, I took time to sit in the heat and study the bare mountains. The thought came to mind about how being vulnerable and exposed - like these mountains - is a place where we can meet honestly with God. With nothing in the way, we can bare the secrets of our heart to him purely and wholly. When we become this open with the Lord, his presence is so near, we can do nothing else but fall down in worship, just as today's scripture explains. Can you imagine how cleansing that could be?

We can all be 'pretenders' sometimes, hiding our hurts so well, until we know that something needs to give or we are going to break down. Thank God we can come to him and surrender those feelings for relief and help. When you do, waste no time in baring your scars and layers for him to see and heal. Come into his presence with singing, and tears. His love and grace is waiting.

Take a moment to present your heart and feel his presence.

Jehovah God, my Healer, I leave nothing hidden before you. I ask you to heal this heart. I take these secrets and leave them in the death valley of your love, and in exchange I present my worship. My pure, honest worship, with thanksgiving. Amen

Big Horn Sheep

The desert bighorn ranges through the dry, desert mountains of eastern CA, much of NV, northwest AZ, and southern Utah.

Leviticus 22:23 NIV
You may, however, present as a freewill
offering an ox or a sheep.

One of the more amazing views in the southwest is the Painted Desert area in Arizona. It becomes even more special when you get to see the big horn sheep lounging around on the colorful hills.

Sheep make me think about the offerings in the old testament, where the Israelites were required to give animals to atone for their sins, and to honor the Lord in many ways. There was one offering called the "freewill" offering. This is a beautiful concept, because it's not about making a sacrifice out of duty, but just because you love and respect the Creator. Just look at everything he's given us! He deserves our sacrifice of worship, and the painted desert seems to be showing us how to do just that. This desolate place doesn't have much to offer; with no shade, no grass, and nothing to harvest, but the many colors and dimensions of the hills are what the desert brings before the Almighty. And, it's stunning.

When we are in our desert places, we may not feel like we have anything to offer in worship, and that's when the freewill offering comes into play. We worship him just because of who he is. Just because we love him. And don't be surprised if this type of worship becomes the deepest, most spirit filled time of your life. It's in the desert places that we dig deep, through all the pain, to reach for the love. The worship itself pushes the pain away, and brings us right into his presence, and we find healing.

My precious Father, I give you my freewill offering, even in the hard desert places. You are worthy. Amen

Desert Monuments

Monuments are the grappling irons that binds one generation to another. ~Joseph Joubert

1 Chronicles 18:3 NIV
David defeated Hadadezer king of Zobah, in the
vicinity of Hamath, when he went to set up
his monument at the Euphrates River.

Monuments in the old testament are mentioned in many different ways. Today's passage mentions how monuments were setup when a King won a battle, to mark the new territory. I think it's a noble idea. What if we setup monuments when we've won a battle (spiritual or otherwise), proclaiming that we now own this space? "See my monument marker? Come no further!" Those defeated enemies are warned that we have conquered, and have no intention of giving back any of the newly acquired territory. Like drawing a line in the sand.

In the southwest, the monuments in the desert are phenomenal. Check out Monument Valley or Arches National Park. These amazing formations stand on the desert floor as a memorial or monument to the past. What are we supposed to remember from the past here? A flood came through and left these monuments in a strangely artistic form, reminding us of a past E. L. E. (Extinction Level Event).

The story of Joshua shares how God told him to be strong and courageous, that the Lord was with him and would help him defeat the enemy he was facing. The people's faith was tested when they were asked to step into the water to cross the Jordan River, and when they acted on their faith, dry land appeared and they walked safely across. Twelve of the strong soldiers picked up rocks in the middle of the river bed as they were going across, and then made a monument on the other side to remember this event. The Lord had delivered them.

In the same way, we can setup monuments that represent victories hard won, and stake our claim that the enemy has been defeated. Whether you setup stones, or simply write it down in a journal, the act of claiming your victory solidifies it. What victory are you claiming today?

Father, thank you for the victories. Help me to be strong and courageous, to claim my win and make my monuments. Amen

Deserts Week Five Reflections and Journaling Points

Slot Canyons: Asking for guidance for the right path to take.

Death Valley: Don't stay in depression. Find a way out.

Bare Mountains: Bare your heart completely to the Lord.

Big Horn Sheep: Make a freewill offering in your desert place.

Desert Monuments: What victories are you claiming today?

Other Reflections

Deserts
Week Six

The Outback

The mysterious vast single stone, that lies at
Australia's heart. Ayer's Rock. Also known as Uluru.

1 Samual 2:2 NIV
There is no one holy like the Lord; there is no one besides you;
there is no Rock like our God.

Visiting Australia has always been on my bucket list. The desert in Australia is quite different than any where else, with its brightly colored sand, and the famous and mysterious red rock sitting in the outback desert.

Ayers Rock is situated in a huge flat desert area, so it stands out as an anomaly and can be seen from a long way off. It's like a beacon for any person or animal lost in the great outback.

Jesus is that rock we look for to find shelter and safety when we feel lost. The more we walk with God, the more we will be looking for him as our relief from life's storms. How will Jesus calm our storms, you ask? By seeking his peace, we let go of the anxieties we are holding on to. We can't hold on to faith and fear at the same time.

Here's what it looks like for me. I start with prayer, and sometimes a few tears. I open my heart to him, and earnestly seek him with my words and maybe some worship too. Songs that have meaning to us, help us to sing spirit to spirit, our spirit to the Holy Spirit. That's when the release comes and those proverbial chains are broken. You feel lighter and something inside has shifted. I'm not saying the problem or issue is instantly solved, although that can sometimes happen. But you know in your heart that God has heard, and somehow he is carrying part of the load. You know he is working things out, and that you are not alone. We may need to repeat this process to get our breakthrough, but it will come.

Today, if there is something that you feel lost about, look for the rock in the desert. Jesus, standing like a beacon offering shelter and relief from your storm. Reach out for it. Sing him a song. Thank him for working things out for you. Find a scripture to stand on, and speak it out over your situation. You'll feel the fear leaving, and your faith growing.

Papa God, help me to look for you in the desert places, like a beacon calling me home. Amen

Bloom Anyway

Water is a deserts' gold. ~ Matshona Dhliwayo

Psalm 63:1
You, God, are my God, earnestly I seek you;
I thirst for you, my whole being longs for you, in a
dry and parched land where there is no water.

There are times when life feels so cracked and dry, it doesn't seem like you can eek out any joy at all. I know the feeling, and I say, bloom anyway! I love this photo that shows the bright blossoms growing through the cracks in the dead, dry desert. Just add a little water, and look what happens. The desert blooms in spite of itself!

What if you let the Holy Spirit pour out the oil of joy on you? What if you gave yourself to fully worship in spirit and truth? What if you rejoiced anyway? But how? How do you do that when your voice is like dry bones? You dig. Deep.

If you don't know how to dig that deep, let me suggest you spend some time in the Psalms. You'll find some songs of David where he is crying his heart out. He digs deep and makes a song to the Lord out of his grief. Let David give you inspiration. You'll notice that so many times he will be crying out to God in agony, but then whispers that he knows God hasn't forsaken him. He knows God is his source, his strength and his deliverer.

When those dry dead times come, dig into the Word and take a deep drink of water from the fountain of God. *"For with you is the fountain of life; in your light we see light."* (Psalm 36:9) Share your light with someone today, and you will sense the oil of joy pouring out. Joy is coming!

Pour out your oil on me Lord. Let me stand under the fountain of life that can only come from you. Let me see your light again Lord. I love you, and I will bloom anyway! Amen.

Desert Cat

The bobcat has adapted to survive in marginal habitats.
~ Arizona-Sonora Desert Museum

Job 39:21-22 NIV
It paws fiercely, rejoicing in its strength,
and charges into the fray.
It laughs at fear, afraid of nothing.

Have you ever spied a bobcat in the wild? Not many of us have. (My friend Wayne got very lucky with this shot.) They are very stealthy animals, and although cats are not mentioned specifically in the Bible, other animals are portrayed with some of the same traits these cats have - fierce, strong, and afraid of nothing.

The bobcat has survived in the harsh desert environments, because they have learned to adapt. That means they find a way, and don't give up. Sometimes we have to press in and find a way too, so we don't give up when life gets hard. So here's another bit of encouragement, because I've been there, and I know; a little encouragement goes a long way.

I've always been a strongly determined person that pushes through things to find a way to get to the other side, but I know that not everyone is like that. It might have been my tough up-bringing that made me a bit fierce, and I'm thankful for that, even though it was hard and I have a few regrets. But regrets don't have to keep us down. What could have been doesn't matter. It's what you do with what you're given that counts.

Please remember, that every moment in your life has made you who you are today, and if it makes you into a fierce, strong person who laughs at fear, then hallelujah! You are God's beautiful and prized masterpiece.

Thank you Father for every moment - even the hard ones - that make me who I am, your uniquely loved child. Amen.

Deep Canyons

As you go through life, you've got to see the valleys as well as the peaks.
~Neil Young

The highest heavens belong to the Lord,
but the earth he has given to mankind.

Paria canyon in the northern AZ desert, is an amazing water way through an incredibly deep canyon. The walls stretch up to eight hundred feet high, and that can make one feel like a tiny ant in the landscape, powerless in the face of Earth's elements, ready to be squashed by the next flow of water coming around the bend.

On the other hand, these places can also bring out a childlike wonder and awe in knowing that all this was given to mankind to steward by an Almighty Creator. Earth belongs to us! A gift from our Father. This perspective changes everything.

In our spiritual desert places, we can get absorbed in the negative possibilities, and not always see what a gift we've been given. Every trial represents an opportunity for growth and elevating our lives. *"Dear brothers and sisters, when troubles of any kind come your way, consider it an opportunity for great joy. For you know that when your faith is tested, your endurance has a chance to grow.." James 1:2-3 NLT*

I know it's not natural for us to feel joy in the middle of trials, but I think we can move toward that experience over time. What if we made a conscious effort to pause and start looking for the joy, asking, "What is the lesson here?", and smile. Can we dare to imagine what it might look like to actually have joy about a trial we are going through? When the deep walls of our trials are closing in around us, what if we look up, smile and say, "Thank you for this gift." Ha HA!!

Lord, help me to remember that your joy is my strength in every situation. Amen

Desert River

Politicians wanted to mine the Grand Canyon for
zinc and copper, and Theodore Roosevelt said, "No."
~David Brinkley

These trials will show that your faith is genuine. It is being tested as fire tests and purifies gold—though your faith is far more precious than mere gold. So when your faith remains strong through many trials, it will bring you much praise and glory and honor on the day when Jesus Christ is revealed to the whole world.

The Colorado River runs for 1,450 miles, starting in Colorado, and then winding its way through hot, dry deserts in Utah, Arizona and California. A famous part of the river passes through the majestic Grand Canyon, a marvel to see. This ancient waterway and the canyon hold knowledge about our planet that only those with eyes to see can capture, although its secrets are there for all to see if they would.

Sometimes that's how it is with our own trials. Hard times can feel like a long twisty road through our lives, leaving scars and deep hurts. And yet they also hold secrets we can learn, if our hearts are willing.

Have you ever heard the saying, "No pain, no gain"? I sometimes think that's how these things work. Think about the pain that Jesus went through to save us. What about the pain all the apostles and Paul went through to birth the church. We are not exempt. We are in the company of noble men and women of the Bible that all went through many trials. How about we turn our cheek and pull ourselves up by the boot straps and join the fight? We have our part to play in Gods' plan. The secret to learn here is that we are bigger and more important to the plan that we may realize.

Today's scripture gives us another glimpse of how precious and valuable these trials really are in preparing us for the future, the day of Jesus' return, and eternity. Our reward is coming, so we need to work through these trials and get every last lesson , grow in our faith, and stay on track.

Lord, I'm standing strong to do my part, and I want to learn the lessons you have for me to develop my faith and prepare for eternity with you! Amen? Amen. Amen!

Deserts Week Six Reflections and Journaling Points

The Outback: How is Jesus your rock.

Bloom Anyway: Digging deep to rejoice in hard times..

Desert Cat: Learning to adapt when life gets hard.

Deep Canyons: Opportunities in our trials

Desert Rivers: Learning lessons and staying on track.

Other Reflections

If you enjoyed this book,
please leave me a review on one or all of
these online bookstores:

www.Amazon.com
www.BarnesAndNoble.com
www.BooksAMillion.com

THANK YOU!

Meet My Jesus

He died for you. (Yes, you.)

Romans 10:9 NIV
If you declare with your mouth, "Jesus is Lord,"
and believe in your heart that God raised him
from the dead you will be saved.

Maybe you already know my Jesus, but I could not close this book without giving you the invitation to receive him into your heart, in case you've never taken that step.

Not sure? Then **let's make sure** you don't go another minute without knowing without a doubt that he knows you and loves you. That he actually died so that you could come into his household and become an adopted son or daughter of the Most High God. Come without hesitation into the life he has for you. A life full of freedom and peace deep in your soul, because you *know* you are accepted just the way you are. Believe, and receive the gift of the Holy Spirit placed in the middle of your heart to intimately know without a doubt *who's* you are.

The story of Jesus is well known; I'm sure you've heard it before. Father God sent his one and only son to be the ultimate sacrifice for us. He paid the price for sin in the world, so we don't have to. It was a horrible death, but then a miracle happened. He awoke from death and was the first to go to be with the Father. But his sacrifice made it possible for anyone who would believe to join him. Not just in heaven, but on a spiritual journey here and now, to grow into the best version of ourselves, and maybe bring a few folks along with us.

It's this easy: If you believe in your heart, tell him directly: "Jesus, I believe You died for me! I believe you were raised from the dead. I ask you to breath the gift of the Holy Spirit on me so I can know you deep in my soul." Now tell someone! Find your tribe of other believers and get connected to a local church. Congratulations on beginning your spiritual journey! Welcome to the Family!

Would you do one more thing? Would you contact me and tell me you met my Jesus? *www.CedarRidgeBooks.com/contact-us*

Mountains Photo credits:

Introduction:	Wallpaperflare.com
Healing Mountains:	†Eder Maioli
Royal Cedar:	Slichter 2005
The Mighty Oak:	Andrew Shelly - Unsplash
Grassy Fields:	Autthaporn Pradidpong - Unsplash
Earth Rhythms:	ted-ielts.com
Mountains Majesty:	Royalty Free Image
Eagleís Wings:	wallpapersafari.com
Secret Places:	wallpaperaccess.com
Surefooted Deer:	Stephen J. Krasemann
Mountain Storms:	Ales Krivec
Natures Wisdom:	Alexander Fattal
A Forest Home:	Sonny Mauricio - Unsplash
Mountain Birds:	hawkmountain.org
Mountain Songs:	wall.alphacoders.com
Hiding Places:	Kentucky Caving
Mountain Meadows:	Raychel Sanner - Unsplash
Deep Truths, Hidden Secrets:	lukasz Szmigiel - Unsplash
Giant Redwoods:	Aaron Logan
Walking in Love:	wallpapersafari.com
Mountain Refuge:	Canada sunset free for use
High on a Hill:	Jean Beaufort
Mountain Pass:	Alan Stark
Mysteries:	PickPik.com Royalty Free
Gold Mines:	Denver Public Library
Moving Mountains:	Robert Krimmel
Restless Spirits:	Samantha Weerasinghe
The Beauty of Nature:	publicdomainpictures.net
Challenging Trails:	mygrandcanyonpark.com
Pine Cones:	FreeImages.com
Mountaintop Moments:	gotmybackpack.com

Waters Photo Credits

Skies Photo Credits

Introduction	Taylor Durrer
Starry Nights	Casey Horner
Sunset Beauty	wallpaperaccess
Heavens Praise Him	Boyd K Packer
Peaceful Skies	Wikimedia Commons
New Day Dawning	allmacwallpapers
The Stars Speak	universe today
Flowing Winds	Shikhar Bhattarai
Promises	Austin Schmid
A Flood of Light	Pikwizaed
Clear Blue Sky	Irina Ward
Morning Light	Wallpapetag
Beams of Light	Public Domain
A Dry Season	Public Domain
Spot Light	Davide Cantelli
Before the Sun Sets	Public Domain
Search Lights	Pixabay
Lightning	Public Domain
Naming Stars	Getty Images
Light Breaking Through	BAonline
A Sign in the Sky	ABC News
Interpreting the Sky	Publicdomainpictures
The Cosmos Praise Him	Wikimedia
Lights in the Sky	Blue Planet High Def Wallpapers
Signs in the Heavens	Blog-Board
Northern Lights	Shashi Tharoor
The Bigger Picture	Wallpx
Shadows in the Sky	Firdia Lisnawati
Sun Dogs	Newsflare.com
Air Waves	wallpapercrafter/ Qwesty
Unique Planets	Hubble Space Telescope NASA

Deserts Photo credits:

Cover	Nate Hovee
Introduction	Jenifoto
Red Rocks	Heber Lopez
Frozen Desert	Jenny Hernandez
Super Bloom	Ron Thomas
Sea of Sand	Lucyna Koch
Sand Storms	AZ Dept of Public Safety
Desert Beauty	Nate Hovee
Desert Mountains	Jack Brauer
Coyotes	Joshua Wilking
Desert Night Sky	David Arment
The Saguaro	Carter Ledford - Unsplash
Desert Sunset	wallpapers.com
Balancing Rock	Wayne Schwetje
Loneliest Road	travel-lingual.com
Road Runners	Ann Newman
Mesquite Trees	Eutoch
Palm Tree Oasis	Benedek
Cactus Flowers	Dillon Pena - Unsplash
Ancient Desert Fortress	Mindaugas Dulinskas
Desert Waves	Mike Jones
Rare Beauty	1930-1945 Vintage Postcard
Slot Canyons	Private Collection
Death Valley	Private Collection
Bare Mountains	Private Collection
Big Horn Sheep	Kevin Griffith
The Outback	**Meg Jerrard**
Bloom Anyway	@ienjoyhiking
Desert Cat	Wayne Schwetje
Deep Canyon	Courtesy Bryce Cyn Natl Park
Desert River	Christin Healy
Meet My Jesus	wallpapers.com

Six Week Devotional Journals
Perfect for Individual or Small Group Study

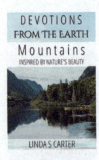

DEVOTIONS
FROM THE EARTH

•Mountains•

Inspired by Nature's Beauty

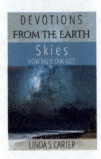

DEVOTIONS
FROM THE EARTH

•Skies•

How Big is Our God

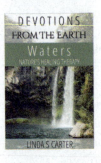

DEVOTIONS
FROM THE EARTH

•Waters•

Nature's Healing Therapy

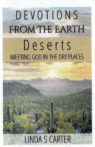

DEVOTIONS
FROM THE EARTH

•Deserts•

Meeting God in the dry places.

DEVOTIONS
From the Earth
Kids Edition

• Bugs & Birds •
• Reptiles & Small Animals •

Amazing images, educational facts and
fun activities about God's creatures,
in a devotional format.

Award winning children's books!

Where to buy:
www.CedarRidgeBooks.com
www.Amazon.com
www.BarnesAndNoble.com
www.BooksAMillion.com

Nature's Peace

Take two minutes in the middle of your week to calm the stress and reconnect. Sign up for our free weekly prayer meditation sent to your inbox.

https://www.cedarridgebooks.com/natures-peace

About the Author

Linda Carter is a wife and mother of one, a grandmother of six, and a lover of Jesus. She has been an entrepreneur for thirty three years as a work-from-home mom, while nurturing her gifts as an author and bible teacher along the way.

Her captivating teachings and writing spring from a life time of walking with God. Becoming a certified California Naturalist was a welcome addition to her study of creation. She enjoys learning how to be a better steward of this amazing world we have been given. Linda sees God's beautiful design in every created thing, with an eye to find the spiritual lessons contained in them.

With years of experience being involved with church ministry, mentoring and outreach, Linda has become a beacon of inspiration for those seeking spiritual growth and empowerment. She also loves teaching others how to appreciate and care for our beautiful planet. Her love for the natural world has played a pivotal role in shaping her unique views on life and spirituality. She shares her insights combined with God's wisdom from a fresh perspective, bringing nature's peace into her writings.

Whether she's found in the pages of her written works, mentoring others through the intricacies of scripture, or exploring the great outdoors, Linda Carter inspires us to step out in our faith, gain knowledge, and develop a deep appreciation for the beauty that surrounds us.

Made in the USA
Columbia, SC
06 March 2025

54729253R00183